CONTENTS

THE
IMAGINARY
VOYAGE

THE
IMAGINARY
VOYAGE

With Theodor Herzl in Israel

SHIMON PERES

ARCADE PUBLISHING • NEW YORK

Copyright © 1998 by Edition °1
English-language translation copyright © 1999 by Arcade Publishing, Inc.

FIRST ENGLISH-LANGAUGE EDITION

"To my Country" by Rahel from Flowers of Perhaps: Selected Poems of Ra'hel, *published by The Menard Press. Translation copyright © 1994 by Robert Friend and Shimon Sandbank. All rights reserved.*

First published in France under the title *Le Voyage Imaginaire*

Library of Congress Cataloging-in-Publication Data
Peres, Shimon, 1923–
    [Voyage imaginaire. English]
    The imaginary voyage / Shimon Peres —1st English-language ed.
      p. cm.
    ISBN 1-55970-468-3
    1. Zionism. 2. Israel—History. 3. Israel—Description and travel.
    4. Imaginary conversation. 5. Herzl, Theodor, 1860–1904.
    I. Title.
    DS126.5.P3913 1999
    320.54'095694—dc21   99-24365

Published in the United States by Arcade Publishing, Inc., New York
Distributed by Time Warner Trade Publishing

10 9 8 7 6 5 4 3 2 1

Designed by API

BP

PRINTED IN THE UNITED STATES OF AMERICA

THE
IMAGINARY
VOYAGE

INTRODUCTION

*T*he Jews have suffered from too much history and not enough geography," one of Theodor Herzl's British disciples, Sir Lewis Namier, was fond of saying. Since the arrival of the first pioneers in the land of Israel during the last two decades of the nineteenth century, and the 1948 Declaration of Independence of the Jewish state, we have made some inroads, however slight, on the matter of geography. But Clio, the muse of history, has not taken that as a reason to forget us — far from it — and what we do and what we say still provide grist for the columns of the world press far more often than they should. The unusual, the paradoxical, and the extraordinary are our daily lot. Whether we be Jews or Israelis, we seem in some way to be a people apart, who always give rise to an endless number of complex questions, the likes of which we would be hard pressed to find in any other nation in the world.

Let me cite one anecdote to prove my point. When I was Israel's minister of defense, I went on an official visit to the United States and was scheduled to be received by my American counterpart, James Schlesinger. It was to be a routine meeting of the sort ministers around the world are accustomed to having. He would hear me out, I would hear him out, and we would end up issuing a communiqué stressing the main points our two countries had in common.

There was nothing happening in the world at that time that indicated our dialogue would not follow that tried-and-true routine to which international relations are often sacrificed.

Upon arriving at his office in the Pentagon, however, imagine my surprise when Schlesinger asked all his advisers to leave the room. As the door closed behind them, he turned to me and without further ado said, "I'd like to talk to you about something that's been really bothering me." Taken aback, I tried to figure out what in the world he had in mind. I racked my brain, casting my mind back over the recent histories of our two countries, wondering what might be the remaining sticking points of our respective foreign policies. But I could not come up with anything that called for such a solemn and serious tone, or the private, confidential nature of our conversation. Already composing in my mind the ultrasecret message I would doubtless have to send the prime minister at the end of our meeting, I stood there on pins and needles. I was prepared for anything — except the question my American colleague suddenly asked.

"My dear Shimon," he said, "tell me in all honesty, do you think Theodor Herzl was right in wanting to create a Jewish state?"

I knew that James Schlesinger, though he had been raised a Christian, was of Jewish origin. But I found most surprising his sudden interest in the author of *The Jewish State*. What would he have said if I had received him in my office in Tel Aviv and opened our discussion by asking, "My dear James, tell me in all honesty, do you think George Washington, Benjamin Franklin, John Adams, and Thomas Jefferson were right in adopting the Declaration of Independence?" He would doubtless have found my question about his country's founding fathers naive and would have had a hearty laugh at my expense.

And yet his question to me about Herzl was dead serious, and he appeared to be awaiting my response with profound interest. I'm afraid, however, that taken aback as I was, all I managed was a string of banalities that I recall were painfully conformist.

Today, I know what I should have replied. I should have said there were two ways of answering his question. The first answer was that the founding of Israel had an inevitability beyond our control. It had its roots in the miraculous. The fact is, Israel abounds in miracles. That first way of responding would have been simply to say, "Yes, Herzl was right, a thousand times right!"

The second way of responding would have been easier, more natural, and also more in keeping with the basic nature of my country, about which David Ben-Gurion once remarked, "Here, if you don't believe in miracles, your head has to be in the clouds."

I would have wished to conjure up a flying carpet and whisk Schlesinger off to share a drink with me at sunset, either at the Cassith Café in Tel Aviv or at the Atarah in Jerusalem in the heart of Ben-Yehuda Street. Sitting on the café terrace, I could have pointed out to him in the gathering dusk several spectral silhouettes, almost unreal, involved in profound and endless discussions, punctuated by raised voices, protests of indignation, and just plain shouts.

I would have explained to Schlesinger that he should not rely on appearances, nor on logic, that terrible scourge of the Middle East, but yield to the facts; those we were seeing in this place were not just ordinary mortals. Tonight, especially for him, a number of historical personages had surfaced, reappeared out of the mists of time. Moses ben Maimon, known as Maimonides, the great Judeo-Spanish philosopher, had conjured up two of his "colleagues" to join him in a discussion: Karl Marx and Herman Cohen. Some who joined them were leading figures of Judaism, others were marginal, even forgotten: Moritz Steinschneider, who in the nineteenth century founded the science of Judaism; Vladimir Medem, the theoretician of the Jewish Revolutionary Autonomist Party, the Bund. And to keep the discussion lively, we were joined by Leon Trotsky, Lenin's close companion, as well as the Jewish-German poet Heinrich Heine, who in his writings sets forth better than anyone else all the torments and contradictions of the modern Jewish soul.

I would have told Schlesinger that every last one of them was arguing about how Herzl should be viewed; all he had to do was listen.

Maimonides would explain that passage from the talmudic treatise set forth by the Sanhedrin, according to which what distinguishes the present world from the messianic period is the "submission of Israel to the nations." When the Messiah comes, things will change completely.

Heinrich Heine, in his own caustic way, would remind Marx that "Judaism is an illness that he would not wish upon his worst enemy," and he therefore found it completely out of line to support any movement, more specifically the Zionist movement, that called for either the preservation or the propagation of this "illness."

Moritz Steinschneider, a kind of connoisseur of the Jewish world, after rummaging in his briefcase would remove from it some sepia-colored photographs of his vast library, which was filled with rare books and manuscripts. He would repeat over and over again the term "assassinate," a word he used to refute the theses of a young Zionist who had come to visit him to win him over to the Zionist cause. "You see," he said to the young man, as he gestured wearily around the room, "if I subscribed to your ideas, all we'd need to do is prepare a proper burial for all these treasures."

And then Marx and Trotsky would chime in, setting forth all the good and valid reasons why they firmly believed in the founding of a classless society, in which neither Jews nor Christians would have any special rights or privileges.

To these remarks Vladimir Medem would immediately lodge a strong protest, convinced as he was that the Jewish question could not be solved within the context of the revolution, and that ex-pariahs had the obligation of preserving what made them special.

After which Herman Cohen, good and decent man that he was, would once again incur the indignation of one and all by muttering his motto, which today has been completely forgotten, "What can I say, I love the Jews, all the Jews. With one exception, and that is the Zionists. What most irritates me about these scoundrels is that they believe in the pursuit of happiness."

I would have had little trouble arranging this very special reunion of some of the most outstanding figures of the Jewish people for James Schlesinger's benefit. Israel is a country whose population is not limited to its current inhabitants but includes generations both past and future. To offer my invited guest such an Areopagus would also have been the best way of responding to his question and satisfying his curiosity.

There was also one other possible answer, it now occurs to me. That is to have conjured up, in the course of the evening I have just described, a middle-aged man crossing the threshold of the Cassith or Atarah and saying to the aforementioned customers gathered there:

"Good evening. I have just heard your various comments and exchanges, which I found fascinating. Allow me to introduce myself: Dr. Theodor Herzl, dramatist, Paris correspondent for the *Neue Freie Presse*, and president of the Zionist Executive Committee. I should like to rectify some of the points you have made and demonstrate that your criticisms have no basis in fact, as I believe our good friend Mr. Schlesinger — whom you had the wisdom to include in your discussions and who is still awaiting a reply to his question — might be the first to agree. The poor man is doubtless unaware of our little Jewish failing, which is to believe that questions are more important than answers. That essentially is what I wanted to tell you."

Whenever I envision that scene, a chill runs up and down my spine, for at the time I was afraid Schlesinger would discover how naive Herzl was in many ways, particularly in the face of the serious problems we had to tackle. Though he was disappointed by the laconic nature of my response during our Washington meeting, James Schlesinger had no idea how much he owes me, and what I saved him from. For I strongly doubt that any of his informants, starting with Herzl, would have provided him with a satisfactory answer. The thorny problem of the Middle East is already complex enough; after the overly subtle and contradictory explanations and comments made by my imaginary assembly, he would surely have come to the conclusion that things were even darker and more mysterious than he had thought, and that might have had negative repercussions, affecting the future relations between our two countries.

Still, I am grateful to Schlesinger for having refreshed my memory and brought back into my mind a man, Theodor Herzl, who was the unjust victim of his own success. An unfortunate intellectual conformism tends to make us too often the prophets of doom and gloom, or those who lead their contemporaries down the dangerous path of expediency, whereas we give short shrift to those who are so tactless as to see the future clearly and fight for a just cause.

Herzl belonged to that latter species, which was damaging to his posthumous reputation, even among his most ardent and enthusiastic admirers. I need go no further than my own example to prove the point.

I was born in Vichneva, in what is today Belarus, which was then under Polish rule, into a deeply pro-Zionist family. To us, Herzl was an exceptional person, a kind of prince in exile or a king without a crown who had pointed out the route his people should follow. No one questioned his prestige or authority. And yet the Zionist world was wracked by profound internal dissensions — those "Jewish wars" that are still going on today, often with tragic results. Partisans and adversaries of the leading lights and theoreticians of the Zionist movement were at one another's throats, fighting and excommunicating to their hearts' content, even as they themselves were being cursed and condemned by the Bundists, the Communists, and the ultra-Orthodox religious party, the Israel Agudat. Among all these vying factions, Herzl was the one major common denominator, which made it easy for us not to take a closer look at him or his views. I have no memory of ever reading, either as a child or an adolescent, his short work *The Jewish State*, published in 1896, or his utopian novel, *Old-New Land*, whereas I devoured the writings of other Zionist thinkers and the novels of Abraham Mapou, including *The Sin of Samarir* and *The Love of Zion*. The reason I had not read Herzl was because his books were for grown-ups. Yet in my mind, I knew that he was my leader — a Jewish king.

After my *alya** to Palestine in 1934, Herzl became a symbol for me. The only notable change was that he was not solely the founder of the Zionist movement but also a geographic landmark. Tel Aviv, the city to which we had moved, had a Herzl Street, and the principal secondary school of the city also bore his name. Don't go looking for any trace of the famous school today: it was torn down in the 1950s to make room for the construction of the Migdal Shalom — the Peace Tower — during the period of a major building boom in the Middle East. So in those days Herzl was overwhelmingly present in our daily lives, but his presence, buttressed by the panoply of Herzl portraits that adorned the walls of shops and apartments throughout the city, paradoxically made him seem extremely remote.

---

* Literally "rise" or "uphill climb," but used in the sense of "emigration."

When I entered public life, I still knew nothing about him, and made little or no effort to fill that gap. All of our lives were filled to the brim with too many demands. We had entered the final phase of our multimillennial dream, which was to become a free people in our own territory, the land of Zion and Jerusalem, and all this was taking place at the time the Jewish world of our childhood and adolescence had just disappeared in a catastrophe without precedent in history, which as we know has all too often been strewn with blood and tears.

In 1946, I returned to Basel as a delegate to the first postwar Zionist congress. That meeting took place in the same city where, forty-nine years earlier, Herzl had gathered together for the first time those in sympathy with his movement and declared, "Wenn Ihr wollt, dann ist es kein Märchen" ("If you desire it, then it will not be only a dream"). We were just emerging from the nightmare of the Holocaust, and during the entire congress I scarcely had time to give any thought to the founder of the Jewish state, or to try and envision what those feverish days in Basel at the end of August 1897 must have been like.

For over fifty years since then I had been promising myself I would atone for that oversight, but life kept getting in the way. The almost constant state of war in which our country found itself until the Israeli-Palestinian peace treaty of 1993, and the various responsibilities that befell me during my many years of public service, had conspired to keep me from devoting any of my time or energy to

renewing my ties with Theodor Herzl. Then came that
meeting with James Schlesinger.

As I was preparing to write this book, I experienced the
same anxiety every morning as I opened my mail. Would
it come today? What I was looking out for was a letter or
calling card, filled with a closely written text. When it arrived, Hannah, one of my two assistants, handed it to me
and said, "Here's a letter from someone who claims he's
Theodor Herzl! He wants you to act as his guide the next
time he comes to Israel. Can you believe it? One more
nutcase! What shall I do? Toss it in the wastebasket?"

She and my other assistant, Ophrah, were both taken
aback, and more than a trifle worried, to hear me reply, "Not
at all. He's an old friend. I've been expecting his letter for
some time now. Cancel all my appointments. Check to see
what day he's arriving so that I can go to meet him at the airport. Unless he is coming by boat, in which case I'll meet
him at the dock. I'll be away from the office for quite a
while. We're going to travel to the four corners of the country, from Nahariya to Elat, from Ashdod to Metullah."

Both women withdrew quietly from the office, shak-
ing their heads in disbelief. But I was dead serious.

Herzl did return and I traveled with him, murmuring
every step of the way that Yiddish sentence that Shalom
Aleichem placed in the mouth of Tevye, his milkman hero
in the stories that inspired *Fiddler on the Roof,* "Ich hob

gehoulemt ein houlem" ("I dreamed a dream"). Together we visited once again a dream in iridescent colors, sought out his original discoveries, or rather his discovery of the most precious legacy anyone can bequeath one's people: a land and a nation. Only the narrow-minded and unimaginative will find this premise off-putting or surprising. Everyone else has long known that in our country the impossible is a way of life.

Today, as yesterday and tomorrow, dreams are the wellspring of our national life. Israel is the only place in the world where the present constantly interacts with the past and the future, where reality can only be understood through the imaginary. This voyage is one proof — among so many others — of that.

Shimon Peres
Tel Aviv, 5759, 1998 – 99

1

THE HILL OF SPRINGTIME

No doubt about it, and Herzl, my traveling companion, was aware of this almost immediately: today, getting from one place to another is quite different than it used to be. In earlier times, when a writer or a pilgrim — be he Jewish, Muslim, or Christian — set out for the Holy Land, his tour took on epic proportions. Not only would he have to brave the often angry waves of the Mediterranean, but there were also the pirates of the Barbary States to contend with, as well as brigands and bandits, and officials whose palms had to be greased. What was more, a voyager had to ride horseback or travel on the back of a mule along dusty, rutted roads, sleep under the stars, or stay at inns where bedbugs seemed to be given more preferential treatment than the guests. He had to brave the dangers of malaria and cope with the sun, the rain, and the icy winds of winter.

Such exploits often ended up bestowing immortality on the traveler, thanks to the publication of a tome in which he described in minute detail the sites he had visited as well as the perils he had faced and the dangers overcome. Thus there came into being a literary tradition in which the authors recounted their "Voyage to the Middle East," which included not only the medieval Jewish travelers Benjamin de Tudèle, Ovadia de Bertinoro, and Meshullam de Volterra, but also some of the great writers of world literature: Chateaubriand, Herman Melville, and Mark Twain, among others.

For those nineteenth-century voyagers, from whom we are separated by only decades — a mere drop in the historical bucket — traveling was not only an adventure but a battle against time. Sometimes one had to wait several weeks for a ship heading to Jaffa from Alexandria, Constantinople, or Beirut. And before they built a railway line between Jaffa and Jerusalem, the trip between that port and the City of David was an excursion that required at least one night's stopover, usually at the edge of the hills of Judea.

But that was not all. The traveler who had arrived from the West discovered little by little a whole new world. He found another civilization, other ways of dressing, eating, behaving, just as there was a whole new architecture to behold and a very different climate to adjust to, somewhere halfway between tropical and European. It was a time when the prospective traveler made sure to include in his luggage, next to the mosquito netting, linen suits made to order by special tailors, and the inevitable pith helmet replete with a white veil.

Today the world has become one big village through which one travels at breakneck speed. It takes no more than a few hours to travel from the center — variously situated depending on one's nationality — to its periphery. Wherever one goes, one finds the same hotels, comfortably air conditioned, one partakes of the same "international menu," which often includes the same food found back home. And, thanks to the miracle of the parabolic antennae, the voyager can, in most places, even see his own favorite TV show. The fax and the telephone keep today's traveler in close and constant contact with his family and colleagues, whereas in times past letters, carefully written and sealed with wax, took several weeks, if not months, to reach their destination.

Things have evolved to such a degree that we no longer "discover" countries the way we once did. In earlier times, we used to arrive, either by land or by sea, in a state of total fatigue. Today, planes touch down and let us off no more than a few miles from the capital, to which we are quickly whisked by bus, taxi, or rental car, without ever setting foot in those ports, which were once prosperous and teeming but today are eerily still, their empty docks waiting in vain for the return of the great passenger liners.

The principal port of entry to Israel is Lod, the Lydda of ancient medieval texts. That was the first surprise awaiting Theodor Herzl. A half surprise really, because his visionary intelligence had enabled him to foresee that in the future Jaffa, as a commercial seaport, would be swept into the dustbin of history. In his utopian novel, *Old-New Land*, which is set in 1923 (that is, two decades after it was written), visitors from the four corners of the earth arrive in Palestine and Jerusalem by train.

With all due respect to Herzl's prediction, Jerusalem's modest train station, located at the edge of the former German section of the city, is not where visitors streaming in from Paris and New York, Johannesburg and Moscow, Tokyo and Melbourne, Amman and Cairo — and, it is to be hoped, sometime in the not too distant future, Baghdad, Damascus, and Beirut — arrive in Israel, but rather at the David Ben-Gurion International Airport at Lod. A far cry from Herzl's arrival in 1897, or mine, thirty-seven years later. For us, Jaffa was the port of entry, both for freighters and passenger liners, whether people were voyaging first class or fourth. In 1921, the German novelist Arthur Hollitscher published a book entitled *Travels through Jewish Palestine*, which became the breviary for tourists worldwide. It began with this sentence, "The reefs of Jaffa are not a metaphor."

The cautionary note was well founded. From earliest times, Jaffa was rightly reputed to be a particularly dangerous port. Between the shore and the high seas was a barrier reef that, whenever the winds were up, was battered mercilessly by the waves. Unable to dock, arriving ships anchored at a respectful distance from the shore. Longboats were dispatched to unload the passengers who gingerly descended the ladders and gangways. And throughout the trip from ship to shore the skies echoed with the terrified cries of the passengers, for the boats were often overloaded as they made their way, bobbing and weaving, around the looming reefs. Accidents, while not frequent, did indeed occur. Part of the problem was that the men who rowed the boats were paid so much per round trip, and thus they tended to take risks.

I often think of those anonymous voyagers who, having reached the threshold of the Promised Land, perished at sea just off Jaffa. It would be hard to conceive of a more terrible, more tragic end: to be literally within striking distance of your ancestral homeland only to perish by drowning. Which brings to mind the fate of Yehuda Halevi, the great Judeo-Spanish poet of the Middle Ages, who sang with such eloquence of Jerusalem in his Sionides. "My body is in the West," he sang, "but my heart is in the East." His poems were composed before he ever set foot in the Promised Land, and when at last he came and saw the proud walls of Jerusalem rising before his eyes, he was so moved he began to recite an elegy he had written, at which point a horseman, either Muslim or Christian — the versions differ — swooped down and killed him. Thus did Yehuda Halevi join the long list of lovers of Zion who lost their hearts and then their lives en route to the Holy Land.

The memory of those who drowned just off Jaffa is mingled in my mind with that of the passengers of the ship *Pisces,* filled with immigrants clandestinely leaving

Morocco. In 1959, the *Pisces* went down just off the Moroccan shores. And then there were of course all those Jews fleeing Nazi-overrun Europe during World War II, who were packed like sardines into unseaworthy old tubs and perished either in the Mediterranean or the Black Sea.

Today, tourists who go to dine at one of the many excellent seafood restaurants in Jaffa probably have no notion of the dramatic and often tragic scenes to which the city was witness in years past. The lapping of the waves against the shore drowns out the laments of those who perished there over the centuries. These souls form a kind of silent and invisible hedge at the entrance to Israel, as if they wish to remind us in their own way that they too are an integral part of a dream they were destined not to fulfill.

And in a sense they did contribute to the building of the city that sprang from the sand centuries after their deaths. In fact, the memory of how difficult it was to arrive by sea at Jaffa, of those terrifying minutes on the longboats, which seemed constantly on the verge of capsizing, explains why the founders of Tel Aviv made a point of building their city with its back to the sea. In their minds, it was not only to cut off all links with the notion of exile, but also because the angry waves of the Mediterranean had been the graveyard of so many of their people.

*

* *

Both Herzl and I could bear witness to the fact that our first, separate contacts with Eretz Israel were rough. I tend to forget the emotion I felt on board ship when I saw, beneath my astonished gaze, the thin strip of land piercing the horizon. It was the Holy Land, the mythical land of Israel that Jews the world over, throughout their interminable exile, evoked at least three times a day in their prayers. To make contact with that blessed earth seemed to me a miracle; to arrive there safe and sound even more so! I can still vividly remember the awe that my mother, my brother Gershon, and I all felt at that moment. And yet, only minutes before, upon first feasting our eyes on that strip of land, which to that moment we had seen only in the few photographs that had managed to reach us in Vichneva, my heart leapt with joy. I was, at long last, actually going to set foot on that blessed land, the only tangible proof of which had till then been the occasional box of Jaffa oranges sent to us by relatives who had emigrated earlier, oranges of a sweetness beyond compare.

Despite all its dangerous aspects, arriving in Jaffa had one distinct advantage: from one's very first steps one could sense the inextricable tangle of peoples and religions living in this corner of the world, as well as the full weight of history in general and that of each people in particular. Side by side lived Jews, Arabs, Armenians, Greeks, not to mention French and Italian missionaries.

Jaffa, one will recall (in Hebrew *Yaffo*, the root of which means "beautiful"), was the city of the prophet Jonah. God had ordered Jonah to issue a warning to the inhabitants of Nineveh, and he had refused, after which he embarked on a ship for Tarshish. A terrible storm came up and the sailors, blaming Jonah for their woes, tossed him into the sea, where he was swallowed by a whale. After three days and three nights, the whale deposited Jonah safely on shore, whence he made his way to Nineveh and fulfilled his mission.

Jaffa was also the Joppé of Greek mythology, the birthplace of Andromeda, the daughter of King Cepheus and Queen Cassiopeia, whose beauty brought down upon her the wrath of the sirens. Humiliated, the naiads — the nymphs of brooks, springs, and fountains — prevailed upon Poseidon, the god of the sea, to bring about a tidal wave and create a sea monster. King Cepheus, consulting the oracle of Ammon, was told that the only way to appease Poseidon was to sacrifice Andromeda to the sea monster. Andromeda was duly enchained upon the enormous rock that faced the city of Jaffa. But before the monster had a chance to feast upon the poor girl, Perseus, the son of Zeus and Danaë, saved her by cutting off the monster's head, which fell into the sea and, again legend has it, formed the rock of Joppé, where the two lovers married and lived happily ever after. What a pity that Perseus, while he was at it, did not see fit to rearrange the harbor of Jaffa!

When both Herzl and I first arrived at Jaffa, even thirty-seven years apart, the port city was already in full decline. Neither the passage of time nor the people who lived there had been kind to the place, which had been destroyed and rebuilt several times. Arabs, crusaders, Mongols, and Mamluks had successively ravaged it, before it was finally conquered by Napoleon Bonaparte. Over the centuries, churches, convents, and mosques had raised their spires and steeples there, but when Chateaubriand visited Jaffa in the nineteenth century, he wrote, with more than a trace of bitterness, "The misfortunes so often visited upon this city have multiplied the ruins one finds there." He added disdainfully that "the city consists of little more than a wretched, circular pile of houses arranged as a kind of amphitheater set into the slope of a high hill."

Chateaubriand, who would later go on to become the French foreign minister, made no mention of any Jewish community there, however small. We do know that in 1173 Benjamin de Tudèle had noted the existence of one Jewish inhabitant, a modest dyer. But it was not until 1820 that the children of Israel came to Jaffa to stay. That year a Jew from Constantinople, a certain Rabbi Yeshaya Adjiman, bought a house in Jaffa, the *dar al-Yahud* (the house of the Jew), which served as a hostel for Jews arriving from Europe and the Mediterranean basin. In short order, Jews from Morocco and Algeria began to arrive in Jaffa, creating the embryo of a Jewish community.

When Herzl arrived in Jaffa in 1897, there were already several hundred Jews from several countries living there, mixed in with the Arab population. The place had a terrible reputation, not only because of its port. Here is his description of what he found:

The narrow streets, which smell to high heaven, are unsanitary and poorly kept up. On all sides one can see nothing but multifaceted misery: indigent Turks, filthy Arabs, fearful Jews, all living in complete idleness, hopeless poverty, without a shred of hope. One's nostrils are filled with the unpleasant smell of putrefaction, the odor of mold and mildew.

What a surprise was in store for Herzl when he saw that same place today. Completely renovated, it has become a kind of Israeli Montmartre.

Several years after Herzl's scathing report, David Ben-Gurion's judgment was equally harsh. Arriving from the Polish shtetl of Plonsk, he wrote, "Jaffa is worse than Plonsk. This is not the land of Israel. I refuse to remain here one more minute." Most new immigrants felt the same way. The filth and decrepitude of the Jaffa houses took them aback; many of them renounced their dreams of remaining in Palestine. They preferred more modern and salubrious cities such as Alexandria or Beirut or, more often, that new Promised Land across the Atlantic, the United States, which during this period became home for hundreds of thousands of Jews. It mattered little what their fate might be in the New World, even if it meant working long hours in the sweatshops of the garment district or hawking vegetables on pushcarts. Within a few years the newcomers would have amassed enough money to move out to the suburbs of New York or Chicago, where there was fresh air to breathe and elementary rules of hygiene were in force.

When Herzl traveled to modern Israel, he had but one desire, and that was to avoid Jaffa at all cost. I planned, therefore, to whisk him off to the model farm school of Mikveh Israel. Founded in 1870 by the Universal Israelite Alliance under the initiative of the Frenchman Charles Netter, Mikveh Israel was the first Jewish agricultural colony in Palestine in the modern era. It was the first place Herzl visited after he arrived in Jaffa a century ago, and it was there, on October 28, 1898, on the eve of the Sabbath, that he fortuitously met, on the Avenue of the Palm Trees just at the entrance of the school, Kaiser Wilhelm II, who was on an official visit.* For years Herzl had been trying to set up an appointment with the Kaiser, to enlist his aid in convincing the Turkish sultan to grant a charter of colonization for the Zionist movement.

Even today, one has a hard time envisioning this strange encounter between a reigning monarch, upon whom the fate of millions of subjects depended, and a simple journalist, which Herzl was at the time. Moreover Herzl dared expound for the Kaiser's benefit his daring ideas, which many people at the time dismissed as little more than a crazy dream. It must have taken an enormous amount of chutzpah to set forth for the emperor his dream of completely transforming Palestine by a massive immigration of Jews.

---

* The Kaiser and his wife, the Kaiserin Augusta Victoria, had landed in Haifa on October 25, 1898. Their initial visit was to the German Colony on Haifa's Mount Carmel, founded thirty years before by the German religious reform movement.

"You have seen this land with your own eyes, your Majesty," Herzl exclaimed. "Would you not agree that it offers itself to mankind, that it cries out for them to come and save it from the sterility and stagnation into which it has fallen?"

To which the Kaiser responded with broad generalities, simply muttering that in his view the country "was in great need of water, a great deal of water."

Both men were right. But the Zionist leader, though caught up in his dream, was in fact being more realistic. He was simply anticipating what would inevitably come to pass. It mattered little whether people took him for a false prophet or a madman. He could not have cared less. In fact, Herzl's successor in the Zionist movement, Chaim Weizmann, was fond of saying, "You don't have to be crazy to be a Zionist, but it certainly helps."

Now, more than a century after Herzl's initial visit to Israel, that madness guided us throughout our voyage. For however much the man was a visionary and a genius, Herzl could not have imagined the changes that have taken place in the interim, changes that, in some instances, drove him almost crazy.

Herzl arrived not at Jaffa but at the Lod Ben-Gurion International Airport, elegant in his black suit and white starched collar, looking only slightly out of date. I swear he didn't look a day older than in the picture that adorned the walls of so many shops and houses in the Tel Aviv of my youth. In the fever of expecting to see old friends and renew old acquaintances, and in the general hustle and bustle surrounding the momentous event, his initial impressions were necessarily vague. He scarcely noted the changes that had taken place. I was glad to welcome him to Israel. Even now, I can still envision him there so clearly it seems I can feel his vitality and curiosity all at once.

Actually, this arrival was a way of paying him back in his own coin, for he uses the same kind of scene in his novel. In *Old-New Land* his hero, Dr. Friedrich Loewenberg, and his mentor Kingscourt are returning to Palestine twenty years after their first visit. The first time they had disembarked at Jaffa. This time they are sailing into Haifa, since at Port Said the two men had learned some astonishing news:

Traffic between Europe and Asia had taken a new route — via Palestine.

"What?" asked Friedrich. "Are there harbors and railways in Palestine?"

"Are there harbors and railways in Palestine?" The captain laughed heartily. "Where do you come from, sir? Have you never seen a newspaper or a timetable?"

"I shouldn't say never, but several years have passed. . . . We know Palestine as a forsaken country."

"A forsaken country . . . good! If you choose to call it that, I don't mind. Only I must say you're spoiled. . . . You could get to Palestine in less time than it would take to tell you about it. Why not make a slight detour if you've a couple of days to spare?"

They headed for Haifa. . . . They stood together on the bridge of the yacht, and stared steadily through their telescopes for ten whole minutes, looking always in the same direction.

"I could swear that that was the Bay of Akko over there," remarked Friedrich.

"I could also swear to the contrary," asserted Kingscourt. "I still have a picture of that Bay in my mind's eye. It was empty and deserted twenty years ago. . . ."

"How changed it all is!" cried Friedrich. "There's been a miracle here."

I therefore believed that Mikveh Israel was the most appropriate place to start, to show Theodor Herzl that our voyage would not unfold as he had thought. To be sure, he could, if he wished, have revisited the places he had gone to more than a century ago: Rehovot, Rishon le-Ziyyon, the City of David. But with the exception of Jerusalem, none of these sites was as important as they appeared to him then. Other places have sprung up that were more worthy of our attention. Visiting the old farm school, which as noted was founded almost three decades before his initial visit, gave him a chance to see immediately what had taken place, though the original gate was still there. In 1897 the school was surrounded by vast orange and lemon groves, as well as by vineyards. Today the school is no more than a verdant space in the near suburbs of Tel Aviv, which local real estate developers look upon with a covetous eye, dreaming of turning it into plots for the upper middle class.

Yet Mikveh Israel is lucky: so far it has resisted

all efforts at encroachment. Not so lucky is the former agricultural colony Sarona, which was founded by German Protestants from the region of Westphalia in 1886. No point in looking for it on today's map: this peaceful village with its red tile roofs belongs to the past. In its place stands Kyriah, the vast administrative and military complex located in the heart of Tel Aviv.

To begin our trip in Tel Aviv was an obligation, a way of paying homage to the genius of my traveling companion. Two cities in Israel owe their names to Herzl. The first is Herzliyya, founded in 1924 by a group of American Jews. Even though it may not be counted among the most important Israeli cities, Herzliyya is nonetheless one of the country's most famous seaside resorts, which over the years has become a rather posh section of Tel Aviv, its waterfront studded with fine restaurants and first-class hotels, which seems a trifle paradoxical. The second is Tel Aviv itself. When *Old-New Land* was translated into Hebrew, the translator, Nathan Sokolow, entitled it *Tel-Aviv: The Hill of Springtime*. As my friend Warren Christopher, President Clinton's former secretary of state, remarked to me a few years ago, Tel Aviv is doubtless the only city on the face of the earth to bear the name of a book that was written years before the city even existed.

And yet Tel Aviv's roots lie deep in our people's collective memory. More than two thousand five hundred years ago there was a Jewish settlement in Babylonia (today's Iraq) that was mentioned by the prophet Ezekiel:

And I came to the exiles at Tel-a'bib, who dwelt by the
river Che'bar.
And I sat there overwhelmed among them seven days.
(Ezekiel, 3:15)

Nor is that the only biblical reference one can evoke on
the subject. Isaiah himself had promised the children of
Israel that the Eternal, their God, would construct for His
people a city built of sapphires, jasper, garnet, and finely
hewn stone.

O afflicted one, storm-tossed, and not comforted,
behold, I will set your stones in antimony,
and lay your foundations with sapphires.

I will make your pinnacles of agate,
your gates of carbuncles,
and all your wall of precious stones.
(Isaiah, 54:11, 12)

Even a cursory look at today's Tel Aviv proves beyond any
shadow of doubt that Isaiah's architectural prophecies
were sorely lacking. Concrete, glass, and steel have replaced his garnet and agate, jasper and sapphire. But only
nitpickers and habitual complainers will make an issue of
it, for those in desperate need of a new roof over their
heads will inevitably opt for the shorter, more pragmatic
solution. Pouring concrete takes infinitely less time than
cutting diamonds or going off in search of rare and

precious stones in distant lands, as Solomon did for the Temple of Jerusalem.

The founders of Tel Aviv were men in a hurry. They couldn't wait to leave Jaffa behind. They felt cooped up in that cramped and noisy village, where the houses were lacking in even the most basic conveniences. Some of them had already moved away to two outlying districts, Neve Tsedek and Neve Shalom, founded in 1887 and 1891 respectively. These however were stopgap measures, for neither place could truly boast of being modern. Besides, both Neve Tsedek and Neve Shalom literally amounted to bedroom communities: those who ended up there had to commute daily to their jobs in Jaffa. Some dreamed of building a city on the sands they could literally see from their windows, a real city, whose entire population, or at least the majority, would be Jewish. People would both live and work in the city they envisioned; it would be modeled after European cities, with broad, paved streets, its houses set apart from one another. There would be public parks and government buildings, downtown areas for commerce, and tree-lined streets and boulevards where the city's youth could congregate. To accomplish that, they would have to cut off all ties with Jaffa, which is precisely what the founders of Tel Aviv did. In 1906 a company was founded called Ahuzat (estate) Bayit (home), literally the Home Estate.

Over the objections of the Pasha of Jaffa, these urban fanatics had managed to purchase several hundred *dounams** of land from a number of Arab families, land that consisted of long stretches of sand dunes, upon which they intended to build the first Hebrew city of modern times. On April 11, 1909, in the presence of a photographer named Abraham Suskin who had come especially to immortalize the occasion, Meir Dizengoff, a Bessarabian Jew who had been named the first mayor of the city-to-be, drew lots to see who would be the proud owners of the sixty-six parcels — a total of thirty-two acres. Each owner was under the obligation to build a small house surrounded by a garden along Rothschild Boulevard, Herzl Street, and Nahalat-Binyamin Street.

In addition to these houses, there were plans for some public buildings as well, in particular the gymnasium, a secondary school that was to bear Herzl's name. A wealthy British industrialist, Jacob Moses, a delegate to the Zionist congress held in the Hague, had donated $10,000 to that end. Virtually nothing remains today of that preliminary sketch of the city. The oldest remaining buildings of Tel Aviv, aside from a scattering of houses in Neve Shalom and Neve Tsedek, date from the early 1920s. One of them is the house known as the Pagoda, which was built in 1925 by the American Joseph Bloch, and was the first private dwelling with an elevator. Another is the house at 16 Rothschild Boulevard, where Meir Dizengoff lived. Today it is a museum whose main room

---

* A Palestinian measure equal to 1,000 square meters.

houses David Ben-Gurion's Declaration of Independence.

In Tel Aviv, you can still see, at the corner of Bograshov Street and Ha-Yarkon, a house on whose façade is a plaque reading: Beit Rahel Friedmann — Rachel Friedmann's house — which reminds us that only a few decades ago there was a shortage of streets. People sometimes had to let the world know where they lived by posting their names on the front of their houses. Despite that, the new city was open to all sorts of innovations. The first movie house, dubbed the Eden, was opened in 1913, and its first offering was, appropriately, *The Last Days of Pompeii*. It was almost obligatory that a house built on sand should show a film depicting a natural disaster, the eruption of Vesuvius and the burying of the fairest cities of Campagna beneath thousands of tons of molten lava and ash.

This sly nod at history didn't escape Theodor Herzl, who like so many of his generation was enamored of classical antiquity. And there was another seeming paradox involving Tel Aviv: the first Hebrew city of our era was also one of the last cities from which, early in this century, Jews were the victims of a general order of expulsion. On March 28, 1917, the Jews of the city were all ordered out of their houses by a decree signed by the Turkish governor of Jaffa, Hassan Beq. The Ottoman Empire had sided with the Germans in World War I, and it was suspected that the sympathy of the Jews lay with the Allies. Hence came the order of expulsion, which was quickly rescinded as soon as General Allenby's British troops arrived on November 16 that same year and took possession of the city.

Thus Tel Aviv has its place in the interminable list of cities that, throughout history, have expelled their Jewish inhabitants. I wondered how to break that news to Herzl. I imagined us seated at the Swing, a fashionable café on Nahalat-Binyamin Street, with as our companion a young Sabra, a native-born Israeli. I knew that if I were to recount that historical incident, I would have to be completely convincing, for neither would have been inclined to believe me. Herzl would have pointedly reminded me that he had conceived his Zionist project so that no Jew would ever again experience the pain and suffering of expulsion or exile. He would have reminded me, too, that the Ottoman Empire was allied to Austria-Hungary, which was where he came from, as did many of the early pioneers who moved to Palestine. The Sabra would have looked at me with a commiserating eye. "I'm sure your facts are confused. That sort of thing might have happened to our fathers during the *galuth*, the Diaspora, but not here. Tel Aviv has always been Jewish!" I would have had to agree with him, at least in part. Tel Aviv has always been Jewish, but it too has suffered the slings and arrows of outrageous misfortune that have been our people's lot.

Anticipating that the expulsion story might anger or upset Herzl, I found it best to change the subject, by telling him how electricity first came to Tel Aviv in 1923, thanks to Phinhas Ruttenberg's Palestine Electrical Corporation. This completely changed the city streets, now flanked with streetlights — the very symbol of ultramodernism. He fully appreciated this story, for he had always been a staunch advocate of electricity, since in his eyes it was one of the ways of solving the problems of the Jews. In *The Jewish State*, he penned these lines, which today strike us as a bit strange:

> I believe that electric light was not invented for the purpose of illuminating the drawing rooms of a few snobs but rather for the purpose of throwing light on some of the dark problems of humanity. One of these problems, and not the least of them, is the Jewish question. In solving it we are working not only for ourselves, but also for many other over-burdened and oppressed beings.

As we can see, Lenin was offering nothing new when he proclaimed, "Communism is the Soviets . . . plus electricity."

The electrification of the city kept pace with its steady growth of population during the years before World War II. In 1925 Tel Aviv had a population of 34,000, which grew to 120,000 ten years later and to 160,000 in 1939. It was no longer a mere subdivision but a real city, and on May 12, 1934, it was granted municipal status with all the rights attendant thereto.

That same year — 1934 — I emigrated to Palestine, which was at that time a British mandate. As I have said, my mother, my brother, and I landed in picturesque Jaffa, filled with the smells of countless spices, and whose inhabitants wore red tarbooshes and baggy, free-floating trousers. No question, I was indeed in the Middle East! But a few minutes later a car drove us off to Tel Aviv, where my father had decided we were going to live. Suddenly we were back in the West! The "veterans" of Tel Aviv were so proud of their city that they had baptized it "Little Paris." I had not known the Parisian capital in those days, but compared to Vichneva, Tel Aviv seemed like a big city and I promptly fell in love with it.

I have followed its explosive growth over the decades. By 1934, the city had spread well beyond its original site, but it was still small enough so that any change, however slight, was quickly noted. For my bar mitzvah my parents gave me a bicycle that I put to good use, setting out each morning to inspect the four corners of the agglomeration, which I viewed as my personal domain. I counted each new tree that had been planted, made due note of the progress on the various building sites, and took personal pride as I saw the new, two-story, whitewashed villas with their little rounded balconies appear out of nowhere. Some of these houses, the brainchild of the famous Bauhaus architects, have steadfastly resisted the ravages of time. Barely more than a child, I acted as if I were the chief magistrate of the city, or the architect responsible for overseeing its construction. I bore very heavy responsibilities on my young shoulders, and there were times when I went so far as to curse out certain buildings that I deemed unworthy of the grandeur of my

"Little Paris." I suspect I was not alone. Every inhabitant of Tel Aviv had his or her own idea of what the city should be, and was more than willing to discuss — argue, more often — the subject with friends and neighbors, prepared if necessary to halt any further construction until the problem was resolved. Had he listened to us, poor Mayor Dizengoff would have reigned over a city composed largely of dreams and fantasies. Fortunately for us all, he preferred to opt for the more practical, more effective course of action.

Despite its relative youth, the city had already spawned its share of tales and legends. We all knew the name of the first thief arrested by the municipal police, a man named Renzel. And there were places of myth such as the San Remo and Palatine Hotels, the latter of which was managed by Lea Rabin's parents. There in 1936 Mayor Dizengoff welcomed the deposed empress of Ethiopia, the wife of Haile Selassie, who had been expelled from her own country and sought refuge in the Holy Land.

I could recite impeccably the current repertories of the three major theaters in town — the Habimah, the Ohel, and the Mataté — and I was proud to know that Tel Aviv already boasted its own opera, which was situated on Allenby Street, not far from the sea. It was also in the 1930s that Toscanini, anxious to show his solidarity with the Jews who were being persecuted, came to direct the Tel Aviv Philharmonic, which Bronislaw Huberman had founded in the late 1920s.

Although it had resolutely turned its back to the sea, Tel Aviv, on the eve of World War II, with a population of over one hundred fifty thousand, had already developed a distinct cosmopolitan air, which became even more pronounced during the war years. Situated not far from the front — battles were raging in Egypt and Libya —Palestine became a vast military base, where soldiers were sent either for training or for R and R — Rest and Relaxation. On both sides of the streets that ran along the shore, bars and pubs sprang up. Beer flowed freely, replacing the sparkling mineral water and fruit juices that we locals were in the habit of consuming in great quantities. Soldiers of all the Allied nations swarmed the streets: British, Australian, New Zealander, South African, Indian, the Polish of General Anders's Army, Free French Forces, Senegalese riflemen, Tunisians, and Lord knows who else. In all, some 2,100,000 Allied soldiers visited Tel Aviv during that war.

Had I wanted to, I could have met Herzl's only direct descendant, his grandson Stefan. Stefan Theodor Neumann was born in 1918, the son of the German industrialist Richard Neumann and of Trude Herzl, the Zionist founder's younger daughter. (Herzl's two other children, Pauline and Hans, committed suicide.) Stefan Theodor was brought up in Great Britain, studied at Cambridge, and, under the name Stephen Norman, joined the British Army and served as an officer in World War II. Both his parents died in the Theresienstadt concentration camp, to which they had been deported in 1942. At the end of the war, in 1945, Stephen Norman made a stopover in Tel Aviv on his way to New Delhi. He spent some time there, making contact with a number of Zionist leaders, all of whom did their best to convince him to settle in Palestine after he had been mustered out of the army. He was offered two high-ranking posts, one in a bank and the other in the Keren Kayemet (the Jewish National Fund) but declined both and returned to London. Shortly thereafter, he was named commercial attaché at the British Embassy in Washington, D.C. He was shy and retiring, a lonely man whose feelings for Britain, his adopted country, were increasingly those of anger, because of Britain's attitude toward the Zionist movement and the aspirations of the Jews to found a Jewish state in Eretz Israel. This, at least, is what Eliyahu Eliat subsequently related. At the time, Eliat was a representative of the Jewish Agency in Washington, and later served as ambassador both there and in London. It was to Eliat that, somewhat mysteriously, Stephen Norman handed a valise containing his writings — both poetry and prose — and various personal documents one day in the fall of 1946. On November 26 of that year, Stephen Norman fell — or jumped — to his death from the Massachusetts Avenue Bridge in Washington.

What must have passed through Stephen Norman's mind during his visit to the city named after the title of one of his grandfather's books? What must he have felt as he walked down Herzl Street, seeing with his own eyes the reality that had evolved out of the ideas put to paper by a man whom he resembled physically to an eerie degree? Was his presumed suicide the result of being afraid he would never measure up to his grandfather? We will never know, for he left no note behind, but I dreaded having to deal with the subject if Herzl were to ask me what became of his children and grandchildren, and whether they were in any way involved in the founding and revival of the Jewish state.

My hope was that we would somehow be able to avoid the subject because our plate was so full of other concerns. For starters, I had to fill Herzl in on the enormous changes that have taken place in Tel Aviv over the past two or three decades. Gone is the time when a child could easily bicycle from one end of town to the other, as I did, and take note of every change that had occurred since the previous day. Today, the trip would take ten times as long, and I seriously doubt that anyone could make it in the course of a single day, let alone record all the urban changes of the previous twenty-four hours.

Whenever I leave Israel for several weeks, or even several days, I am always astonished — and sometimes disoriented — by the changes that take place in the short time I am away. The street names remain reassuringly the same: Sheinkin, Ibn-Gvirol, Montefiore, Balfour, Arlozoroff, and others. But as I make my way through the city, I note that one old familiar two- or three-story building has given way to an apartment house, that a whole cluster of houses has been torn down and in its place has sprung up a spanking new shopping center, with the bright lights of its stores and boutiques burning far into the night.

The Migdal Shalom, the Peace Tower, was for a long time the tallest and most imposing edifice in the Middle East. Today it cuts a poor figure next to the new Diamond Exchange, a gigantic amalgam of concrete, metal, and glass, which soars heavenward, proving, to me at least, man's innate and enduring desire to recreate the Tower of Babel, those ziggurats so near and dear to our ancestors' hearts. Nor is the exchange the only example of futuristic architecture that Herzl found along the banks of the Yarkon. A mere half century ago, Meir Dizengoff's city prided itself on the houses constructed according to the plans of the Bauhaus architects Mies van der Rohe and Le Corbusier, who thrived on innovation. I wondered what he would say when he saw what has supplanted the old Tahanah Merkazit — Central Station — which Tel Avivians loved to grumble endlessly about because they found it so cramped and dirty? Where it once stood now sits the new central bus station, a super-modern passenger-liner edifice of stone and glass, replete with elevators and escalators that give it the look of an enormous launching pad to distant stars. As we toured the building, I had trouble reminding myself that this is still Tel Aviv.

The village of the 1940s and 1950s has turned into a metropolis whose history is written in the future. Past and present are barely distinguishable. Tel Aviv is one of the rare cities of the world that remains unfinished, a city where the term "to construct" does not mean only to re-furbish or preserve a historical center frozen in the patina of centuries past. I am convinced that Herzl liked this city, despite the fact that it has neither the frosty and haughty charm of Vienna nor the venerable aspect of Naples or Rome. He felt quite comfortable here, where it takes no more than a few seconds to go from the West to the Ori-ent and back again, where, just as quickly, you move back and forth between the nineteenth and twentieth cen-turies, where the smell of spices mingles with that of ef-fluvia of a postindustrial society, and where a cart drawn by a clearly undernourished horse is reflected in the win-dows of a skyscraper.

*

*   *

This extraordinary juxtaposition of periods and cultures, however, is not all positive. There is also a dark side to Tel Aviv, one that I found difficult to show or describe to my traveling companion. Only four or five years ago I would have been pleased and proud to take him to the Mu-nicipal Building, which was built not far from the site of the former German colony, Sarona. The building faces the Kings of Israel Square, the center of Jewish public life. But since November 4, 1995, I cannot view that place in the same way, for it was on that day that a young Israeli extremist, Yigal Amir, a student at Bar-Ilan University, committed an irreparable act: he killed the prime minister, my friend Yitzhak Rabin, assassinated him before my very eyes, for no other reason than that Rabin had opted for the path of peace. How could I explain that unthinkable act to Herzl, as I tried to tell him why the Kings of Israel Square is now called Yitzhak Rabin Square? Later on I would have occasion to come back to that tragic page of our history, but I could not conclude our visit to Tel Aviv without honoring this storied site.

In fact this city, forward looking as it is, is also acutely and painfully aware of the fanaticism of another age that still prowls its streets. It tries to cope with evil by seeking escape in festive nightlife. That is how people prepare themselves for, and arm themselves against, madness.

There is a common saying that while Jerusalem prays and Haifa works, Tel Aviv plays — or at least goes through the motions. That is the city's own special way of taking life seriously — as if it still does not quite believe it has somehow managed to survive and is very much alive and well. There are some streets that remain crowded twenty-four hours a day, and you can find a number of grocery stores that stay open around the clock. You can stop on your way home from late-night get-togethers at the cafés along Dizengoff Street to replenish your stock of food and drink, or buy newspapers and cigarettes. With its bohemian air, its taste for the unusual and provocative, Tel Aviv is doing its best to imitate Hemingway's Paris. Even during my adolescence, Tel Aviv competed with Beirut for the title of "Little Paris." Today I think it safe to say that this city, created by a handful of pioneers, has become the undisputed nightlife champion of the region, an all-around lively city that is the marvel of tourists who take the time to spend a few days, or even a few weeks, here.

I had no idea whether Herzl would appreciate the pleasure of today's Tel Aviv nightlife. I had a hard time picturing him dancing to some disc jockey's rock 'n' roll, or taking part in a rave on one of the converted docks at Jaffa. I strongly suspected that he would have preferred the grand balls given by Viennese aristocrats in their sumptuous palaces. I reserved an evening for him at Rishon le-Ziyyon, a place he had last visited roughly a century ago. This once modest village a few miles from Tel Aviv has now become a large city. Rishon played an important role in the genesis of the Zionist movement, something one would be hard pressed to learn from its contemporary streets and buildings. It is not a place whose stones, weathered by the passage of time, bask in the bright sunlight of history. And yet, what events have taken place since the city was founded in 1882 by immigrants from Russia, Poland, Romania, and Yemen! It was here that the first modern synagogue was built in the land of Israel; it was here that the first kindergarten was opened where Hebrew was the language taught. In 1898, my traveling companion spent several hours here, grumbling about the tight control exercised on its inhabitants by the local representatives of Baron Edmond de Rothschild, who had taken the colonists under his financial wing. In their early days the settlers, inexperienced farmers beset by malaria-bearing mosquitoes from the swamps on which they were building, had barely survived. Thanks to Rothschild's advice and administrative know-how, however, the settlement took hold and its inhabitants went on to plant successful vineyards, using French stock brought in 1887. It now produces the Israeli equivalents of French Beaujolais, Bordeaux, and Burgundy. This extraordinary success did not however come about without a fair measure of paternalism, to which the colonists responded by grousing, whenever anything went wrong, "Habaron yeshalem!" ("The baron will pay for that!") For them, as for so many thousands of their fellow Jews of the time, Rothschild was their own special banker, whose wealth they envied and whose generosity they constantly solicited.

Our evening at Rishon le-Ziyyon nonetheless took place without the Rothschilds. I spent the evening taking my companion to the site of the former cultural center, a fancy term for a modest little shanty that was barely capable of holding more than a few dozen people. But within those hallowed walls the hymn of the Zionist movement — which later became the Israeli national anthem — "Hatikvah" ("The Hope"), was composed and performed for the first time.

Joining us was that song's composer, Naphtali Herz Imber, who made the evening lively (although I must confess his unpredictable nature had given me some cause for concern). Israel is the only modern state whose national anthem was composed by a beatnik (before that designation existed), a polyglot adventurer, a sometime poet, a drinker of Rabelaisian proportions, and a ladies' man, whose drunken bouts and countless love affairs, grist for the local gossip columns of the time, earned him the undying wrath of the orthodox and right minded. When they made Imber they broke the mold: he was truly the spiritual father of Tel Aviv's bohemian world during the 1930s and 1940s — and still is today. The current bohemian crop would have been delighted to hear him declaim in Hebrew his translations of Omar Khayyám's fiery poems, extolling the virtues of wine and forbidden love. And this same man composed the solemn song whose notes mark all the great events of the history of Israel. For me, as for millions of Jews around the world, "Hatikvah" is a melody I cannot hear without feeling enormous pride. I like the fact that it was composed by a follower of François Villon, who was not exactly a paragon of virtue himself. It was as if Imber wanted to put us on guard against any kind of extreme nationalism or chauvinism, as well as warn us against any fetishistic use of national symbols.

In addition to Imber, I brought back another citizen of Rishon le-Ziyyon, a man who lived there in the 1880s, Dr. Maze, the local physician. Herzl and he had had long discussions at the time of Herzl's first visit to Israel. For some strange reason, Maze had become convinced that Herzl's secret goal was to convert the Jews to Protestantism, and he went about slandering him to all who would listen. Herzl for his part had been extremely excited by the picture of Palestine Maze had drawn for him, and was especially interested in what the good doctor had to say about the malaria ravaging the country. So impressed was Herzl by his conversations with Maze that in *Old-New Land*, he uses him as a model for his Professor Steineck, in whose mouth Herzl put Maze's words. Steineck, who had vowed to devote his life to conquering malaria, had no intention of confining his efforts to the Holy Land itself:

"That is to say, I hope to find the cure for malaria. We have overcome it here in Palestine, thanks to the drainage of the swamps, canalization, and the eucalyptus forests. But conditions are different in Africa. The same measures cannot be taken there because the prerequisite — mass immigration — is not present. The white colonist goes under in Africa. That country can be opened to civilization only after malaria has been subdued. . . ."

Kingscourt laughed. "You want to cart off the whites to the black continent, you wonder-worker!"

"Not only the whites!" replied Steineck gravely. "The blacks as well. There is still one problem of racial misfortune unsolved. The depths of that problem, in all their horror, only a Jew can fathom. I mean the Negro problem. Don't laugh, Mr. Kingscourt. Think of the hair-raising horrors of the slave trade. Human beings, because their skins are black, are stolen, carried off, and sold. Their descendants grow up in alien surroundings, despised and hated because their skin is differently pigmented. I'm not ashamed to say, though I be thought ridiculous, now that I have lived to see the restoration of the Jews, I should like to pave the way for the restoration of the Negroes."

It pleases me that in his utopian world, Herzl focuses on Africa, that riven and martyred continent in which the worst tragedies coexist with hope and an extraordinary will to live. I would love to have brought Herzl together with Nelson Mandela — he who also, after much personal pain and suffering, was able to liberate his country. The two men have a great deal in common, notwithstanding the reservations recently formulated by the South African president regarding certain aspects of Zionism. In any event, we should recall and applaud Herzl's concern about Africa, that continent on which are scattered so many branches of our own people, from the mysterious Tombouctou to the Cape, from Nairobi to North Africa, and Egypt of course, the land where Moses was born.

Today, the doctors who followed in Maze's footsteps no longer practice in Rishon le-Ziyyon or in Tiberias, but work in the country's various research universities: Jerusalem, Tel Aviv, Haifa, or Beersheba. And when my companion and I stopped off at a place he had briefly visited before — Rehovot — he had a hard time recognizing it. During his earlier visit Herzl had been amazed to see Jews riding up to meet him on horseback, then putting on a special performance for him. "They reminded me," he wrote, "of the cowboys of the American Far West that I saw in Paris one day." He was referring to the visit Buffalo Bill and Sitting Bull made to the French capital, where they put on a show depicting life on the American prairies — and profited from the Europeans' romantic visions of the new world. Long gone are the Jewish cowboys of yore, their dusty roads having been replaced by paved arteries. The entire city of Rehovot is devoted to science, and has been ever since the founding of the Chaim Weizmann Institute of Science in the 1930s. The institute enjoys the highest reputation worldwide. The pioneers of yesteryear have exchanged their coarse Russian shirts for the researchers' white labcoats, and today's inhabitants are more interested in particles than saddle horses.

All of this proved of slight importance. Herzl was as comfortable with them as he was with the proud Jewish riders of the past. He listened to them just as patiently, and with just as much interest, while they explained the finer points of their research. But after a while his mind wandered elsewhere, as he began to think of the next stage of his itinerary, Jerusalem, the Holy City, always and forever the epicenter of the Jewish soul.

2

THE WALLS OF JERUSALEM

*A*fter considerable hesitation, I suggested to Herzl that we go to Jerusalem by train. I have to confess that in today's Israel, this means of transportation is neither the most rapid — far from it — nor the most comfortable. Contemporary travelers, for whom time is money, generally prefer to go from Tel Aviv to Jerusalem by bus or collective taxi, which takes a little under an hour. The Tel Aviv train station, at least the one that serves Jerusalem, is located on the outskirts of the city, which doesn't make things any easier.

And yet by taking the train we were tipping our hat to History, for when my companion came to Eretz Israel the first time, that is how he traveled from Tel Aviv to the City of David. After his meeting with Kaiser Wilhelm II at Mikveh Israel, Herzl and several of his disciples boarded the Jerusalem line of the Ottoman Society Jerusalem-Jaffa & Environs Railroad. The short trip filled

Herzl with mixed feelings. First of all, the train was considerably late and he, as a good European, was a stickler for punctuality. Further, as luck would have it, they had left on a Friday afternoon and by the time they arrived in Jerusalem it was well after sundown on the Sabbath. So as not to upset his companions, who were strict Orthodox, he walked to his hotel, a good half hour away, cursing his bad luck the whole way, for autumn nights on the hills of Judea run to extremely cool if not cold. In light of the enormous tasks that lay ahead of him, he must have mused, wouldn't it be just my luck to come down with a cold that would keep me bedridden for several days!

The memory of that experience remained so clearly etched in his mind that Herzl made the renovation of the Palestinian railway network one of the primary goals of the "New Society" he set forth in his novel — with emphasis on improving both the speed of the trains and their punctuality. I have always wondered whether he intended to take a pot shot at the Rothschilds, the Pereires, and the Poliakovs, all those Jewish multimillionaires of the day who had financed the construction of railway systems in France, Germany, Austria-Hungary, Russia, and Turkey, but had stubbornly refused to put up a penny to back his dream of a Jewish state. That "railroad obsession" in his utopian novel is in one sense a way of venting his frustration, a childish act of revenge for the humiliation he had been made to suffer.

Since I knew how strongly Herzl felt about the matter, I was hesitant to show him the state of our modest railway system. I knew ahead of time what he would say about our trains, which are not exactly the Orient Express. But I opted for the train in order to show him how mistaken he had been on the question of language. Herzl had proposed making German the official language of the Jewish state. To justify his choice, he used the railroads. "Who among us," he was fond of asking, "knows even enough Hebrew to buy a train ticket in that tongue?" As we bought our tickets, he readily admitted how wrong he had been in making that statement.

I didn't hesitate to make this point to him, for I was fully aware how important this next stage of our journey was. Herzl had come away from his earlier visit to Palestine with mixed feelings about Jerusalem, ranging from complete enthusiasm to total exasperation. That first Friday evening, after he had tardily arrived at his hotel, he noted feverishly in his *Diary:*

> All I can do is look out of the window and conclude that Jerusalem is magnificently situated. Even in its present decay it is a beautiful city; and, if we get in here, can become one of the finest in the world.

Two days later, after he had strolled through the Jewish quarter of the Old City, and having climbed up to the Mount of Olives, he wrote:

> I am firmly convinced that a splendid New Jerusalem can be built outside the old city walls. The old Jerusalem

would still remain Lourdes and Mecca and Yerushalayim. A very lovely beautiful town could arise at its side.

Like millions of other visitors before and since him, Herzl was overwhelmed by the strange majesty of the place, about which the Talmud proclaimed that nine of the ten measures of beauty sent down to earth had been bestowed upon it. And yet, in other passages of his *Diary*, he tends to judge the city very harshly and pessimistically, and many of his remarks would offend more than one Jewish nationalist today. In his entry of October 31, 1898, at a time when he did not know whether or not Kaiser Wilhelm II would grant him a further audience, he writes, literally in a state of rage:

When I remember thee in days to come, O Jerusalem, it will not be with delight.

The musty deposits of two thousand years of inhumanity, intolerance, and foulness lie in your reeking alleys. The one man who has been present here all this while, the lovable dreamer of Nazareth, has done nothing but help increase the hate.

If Jerusalem is ever ours, and if I were still able to do anything about it, I would begin by cleaning it up.

I would clear out everything that is not sacred, set up workers' houses beyond the city, empty and tear down the filthy rat-holes, burn all the non-sacred ruins, and put the bazaars elsewhere. Then, retaining as much of the old architectural style as possible, I would build an airy, comfortable, properly sewered, brand new city around the Holy Places.

That impression was so deeply embedded in him that he passed it on to his protagonist Friedrich in *Old-New Land*. For Friedrich, Jerusalem is little more than noise and stench, a kingdom of beggars and merchants.

The truth is, these somewhat pessimistic descriptions of the city on the part of Herzl, or rather of his character, have to be taken with a grain of salt. To me, they emanate from what I call "Jerusalem syndrome," which affects many Jewish visitors. I am not referring to the "Jerusalem syndrome" the press keeps harping on, referring to those tourists who often, during their stay in the Holy City, act as if they are the Messiah whom God has chosen to tell the entire world that punishment is at hand, and that it will be inflicted upon every man, woman, and child. The "Jerusalem syndrome" I'm referring to is the obsession so many Jewish voyagers have about using the Book of Lamentations to describe the city of David. It is as if they felt in the depths of their soul the pain of the true believers when they celebrate, every ninth day of the month of Ab, the destruction of the Temple.

It matters little what the reality of contemporary Jerusalem may be; for these visitors it can never be anything else but the humiliated city, the destroyed city, the city whose reconstruction they await on the Day of Judgment. From that viewpoint, Herzl was infinitely more Jewish than he was aware — and a little like Kafka's compatriots, about whom the author of *The Trial* was fond of saying, "For some mysterious reason, they know a lot more Yiddish than they pretend."

During that earlier stay in Jerusalem Herzl acted as if Eretz Israel was, and would always be in his eyes, "the land with a broken heart," and Jerusalem the epicenter of that desolation. In fact, this particularly pessimistic vision was in large measure unjustified, because even then the City of David was in the midst of an unprecedented renewal that would continue throughout the twentieth century. That is an incontrovertible fact that needs to be emphasized, if only to give due credit to the artisans of that renaissance who, starting in 1830, had begun to awaken the city from its long torpor.

There are a number of examples to back that up, starting with the fact that during this period a number of countries opened consulates in Jerusalem: Great Britain, Prussia, France, Austria-Hungary, and Russia. All had permanent missions in the city, whose purpose was to look out for the security and well-being of their citizens, who were becoming increasingly numerous, pilgrims or tourists lured by the mysteries of the Orient, or those who had come to stay, such as those German peasants from Würtemberg, who founded in Jerusalem the Moshava Germanit, the German Colony.

Among all those nations participating in the renaissance of the City of David, France, who had long supported Christian groups in the Middle East, was in the forefront, partly because it had been granted favorable status. During the Crimean War, France had sided with the Turkish sultan. To show his gratitude to Napoléon III, the sultan offered, in memory of Napoléon Bonaparte —

who had been the unfortunate loser in the siege of Acre —
the beautiful church of Saint Anne, which was put under
the jurisdiction of Cardinal Lavigerie's White Fathers.
Thus France was able to build on land ceded to it by the
Ottoman authorities the combination monastery and hostel under the name Notre Dame de France, situated just
opposite the walls of the Old City and contiguous to the
world-famous Saint-Louis Hospital. Although he was extremely knowledgeable about France, Herzl remained
unaware of this state of affairs, or rather preferred to in-
terpret it in his own way. Seeing that the grill of the gate
that leads into the tombs of the ancient kings of Israel
displayed — and still displays today — the letters RF
(République Française), he noted sadly:

> We visited the tombs of the Kings, which were on the land
> that had once belonged to a French Jew, Pereire, who
> bequeathed it to the French government. Which goes
> to show how impossible it is for Jews ever to own any-
> thing.

His remark was unjust given that in the nineteenth century the Sublime Porte had lifted the restriction under
which foreigners — in essence Christians and Jews —
were formerly forbidden from buying land in Palestine.
In fact, the opportunity to buy land was the impetus behind the creation of whole new sections of Jerusalem,
which sprang up beyond the parameters laid down by Süleyman the Magnificent, sultan of Turkey, in 1538. The

construction of these new areas was entrusted to Abraham Castro, the master of the treasury and *naggid*, or head of the community, of the Egyptian Jews.

Taking advantage of the Ottoman authority's favorable rulings, Sir Moses Montefiore, the greatest Jewish philanthropist of the day, whose generosity exceeded even that of the Rothschilds, was the first to have a series of houses built opposite Mount Zion, the Mishkenot Shaananim (Dwellings of the Blessed), intended to offer Jews of the city better and healthier housing. Shortly thereafter, above this little cluster of handsome dwellings, which today are used to house official guests of the municipality, he had built a windmill, whose elegant silhouette dominates the Mishkenot. Montefiore also funded four sections on the outskirts of Jerusalem that bear the names Yemin Moske, Zikim Moske, Okel Moske, and Kyriat Moske.

The growth of the Jewish population of Jerusalem throughout the nineteenth century was, moreover, the impetus for the creation of other sections of the city, such as Mahane Israel, Nahalat Shiva, or Mea Shearim.

Thus, the desolate picture of Jerusalem that Herzl painted in 1898 is a far cry from today's reality. His pessimism and ill humor stemmed in large part from the tense atmosphere that prevailed during his stay in the City of David. He was hoping and praying to obtain another audience with Kaiser Wilhelm II, but the emperor's advisors, especially his foreign minister, Bernhard von Bülow, did everything they could to prevent it, arguing that to grant such a favor to Herzl would aggravate the Ottoman authorities, who had very strong feelings about their sovereignty in the Holy Land. What was more, far from welcoming Herzl as a savior, the leaders of the local Jewish community were openly hostile to him. In fact, the Great Rabbi of Constantinople had written to his counterpart in Jerusalem, requesting that Herzl be excommunicated.

While they did not go that far, the Jews of the City of David made a point of forbidding the Zionist leader from joining them under the Arch of Triumph that had been erected in honor of the Kaiser's entrance into the Holy City. Nursing his humiliation, Herzl was made to cool his heels at the house of one of his followers, a man named Stern, who lived at 18 Mamilla Street, next to the Jaffa Gate.

Not until November 2 did Kaiser Wilhelm II agree to see him. Their meeting turned out to be routine and perfunctory, leaving Herzl upset and bewildered. All the hopes he had harbored that Berlin would declare itself in favor of the Zionist movement came crashing down, which led him to change his plans and return to Europe as fast as he could. In short, this first visit to Jerusalem left Herzl with bitter memories, and it took all the persuasion and diplomacy at my command to make sure his second visit was more auspicious.

*

* *

It took some doing on my part to make Herzl understand that German is not the language in which the arrival of the Sabbath is chanted. Rather than try to broach the unimaginability of Shoah — a subject I reserved for later — I limited myself to telling him that, contrary to his predictions, Hebrew is not only the language used in Jewish liturgy, but also the official language spoken every day by virtually the entire population of the country. To make him understand how this happened, I gave him a blow-by-blow description of the extraordinary struggle by the father of modern Hebrew, Eliezer Ben-Yehuda, to resuscitate the sacred language and transform it into a living idiom, a struggle that, as his son describes it, he had decided, no matter what, to undertake shortly after he had married:

> During his honeymoon, my father took my mother on a pleasure cruise down the Danube. Just as their ship was passing through the Iron Doors, he said to his bride, "The Iron Doors are the symbol of will power; that is why I chose this spot to inform you that from now on I intend to speak to you only in Hebrew." My mother, who had only the most rudimentary notions of Hebrew, thought he was joking, but he was in fact dead serious. And from that day on he made my mother his first student: he spoke to her only in Hebrew.

Ben-Yehuda's decision had serious consequences, since the Orthodox Jews of Jerusalem, where Ben-Yehuda lived, were up in arms about the secularization of Hebrew and subjected him to all sorts of persecution; to them, He-brew could only be used for prayer and study of the sacred texts. Their hostility was directed not only at Ben-Yehuda himself but also at his son. Itamar Ben Avi was the first person of the modern era whose mother tongue was the language of the Bible, and his memories of the experience are grounded in bitterness. He had nobody his own age to talk to, and his father's efforts to console him came to naught:

> Since I had no friends my own age, to keep me from feel-ing completely isolated my father bought me a dog. One day I was out walking my dog and, without meaning any harm, I said a few words to him in Hebrew. Some Ortho-dox Jews who were passing by heard my words and were scandalized — to such a degree that they picked up some stones and began throwing them at my dog. They ended up stoning him to death. My father built a little monument to the martyred dog, the first victim of the Hebrew lan-guage.

I wasn't overly worried. On the question of Hebrew, I was quite sure I could not only satisfy Herzl's curiosity but convince him of the ultimate wisdom of this linguis-tic evolution. He wouldn't take umbrage so long as he knew that that linguistic shift was in no way a decisive and complete refutation of the way he imagined the Jerusalem of the future. On other subjects, however, I knew I would have much more trouble not disappointing him or suffer-ing the sting of his wrath. When we proceeded together to the Kotel, the Wailing Wall, I feared he'd confront me with what he wrote when his heroes first came upon the place, "The repellent spectacle of the beggars, for whom prayer was a ritual, was painful to see." For today there are still beggars in the vicinity of the Wailing Wall, some of whom chant monotonously as they accost the passersby murmuring in Yiddish, "Yidden, hat rahmouness, macht a mitsve" ("Jews, have pity, do a good deed").

To explain and justify the presence of beggars, the schnorrers, at today's Wall wasn't difficult. What was harder to explain, though, was the presence of so many armed soldiers patrolling the holy sites of Judaism, Christianity, and Islam: the Kotel, the Church of the Holy Sepulcher, and the Haram al-Sharif, the esplanade of the Mosque, which is adjacent to both the Dome of the Rock and the El Aksa Mosque. When I told him that such a blatant show of the military was the result of constant tensions among the various religious and political elements of the Holy City, he reminded me how one of his fictional heroes responded when asked how the inhabitants of the New Society had dealt with the problems of the Holy Places: "When it comes to the Holy Places," says Herzl's hero, "there can be no question of private ownership. Religious feelings are more easily satisfied if these sacred sites belong to no one exclusively but are under the jurisdiction of a single temporal power."

Jerusalem today is a far cry from that idyllic solution of which Herzl dreamed. His plans to internationalize the city would have raised a terrible hue and cry from most if not all current-day Israeli politicians, no matter what their stripe, since Jerusalem, from 1967 on, has been reunified and become the eternal capital of the state of Israel. Herzl no doubt figured this out for himself, simply by noting the absence in Jerusalem of any Palace of Peace, which he had envisioned as being the center of philanthropic activities, a kind of League of Nations before its time. He had described the Palace as being located in the heart of the city, symbolizing the spirit, at the time it was built, that had informed the members of the Zionist movement of the New Society.

I hope with all my heart that I will live to see the actual building of his Palace of Peace, though I think it fair to say that we have not been entirely unfaithful to the various peace missions that Herzl foresaw as an integral part of the Jewish state. I can cite chapter and verse detailing the different forms of international cooperation that have evolved, in the realm of agriculture and irrigation, in conjunction with the most backward countries of the planet. I told him about the various humanitarian missions we have carried out with a number of countries — including some with whom we had no diplomatic relations — whenever catastrophe struck. Thus at the time of the Soviet Chernobyl nuclear disaster — that city once having been home to an important Hasidic dynasty — we offered our medical help and services, despite the fact that Israel and the then Soviet Union were at odds politically. And we did it again in 1988, when Soviet Armenia was rocked by terrible earthquakes. I also cited the case of the Israeli doctors dispatched to the heart of Africa, to Rwanda and neighboring countries, to help the victims of the endless butchery that took place following the death of Rwandan president Juvénal Habyarimana in April 1994.

I knew that Herzl might reproach us for not having built his cherished Palace of Peace. And I was all the more uncomfortable in his presence, knowing that Jerusalem, although it offered to his eyes the spectacle of a unified city today, is nonetheless crisscrossed by an invisible frontier fully as effective as the east-to-west wall constructed by the Jordanians after 1948. The various walls of Jerusalem are infinitely more solid than people think, and are not limited to those perimeter walls built by Süleyman the Magnificent.

To be sure, those walls are also still standing, and the sun continues imperturbably to beat down upon their ocher stones winter and summer. They encircle the Old City, the part that Herzl planned to reserve for the use of religious institutions and charitable organizations. Today the city is not lacking in either of these categories, quite the contrary. In the few square miles that make up the Old City, there is a concentration of religious and charitable institutions unequaled on the face of the earth. Churches, monasteries, synagogues, mosques, and yeshivas are gathered there, as well as foundations that dispense to the faithful of various beliefs the subsidies they need to pursue their pious studies and research.

This Old City, which some people refer to as the "Arab city" because Muslims have long been the majority of its inhabitants, is actually a veritable jigsaw puzzle of different religions and ethnic groups, many if not all of which have been in conflict since time immemorial. Each has abrogated unto itself various plots of land, various streets, sometimes resorting to force, sometimes to persuasion, to gain its ends. Today's tourists, on their first trip to Jerusalem, already groping to make sense out of this religious and ethnic hodgepodge, have a great deal of trouble distinguishing the Armenian section from the Greek Orthodox, or the Jewish section from the Arab, despite the differences of language and dress. Old-time Jerusalemites, on the contrary, know instinctively just where one section ends and another begins. They know that up until such and such a street they are in friendly territory, and that at the end of this or that dead-end street, which goes unmarked, they have crossed into hostile territory.

These invisible frontiers shift with the years and the centuries, as if the configuration of Jerusalem was subject to some mysterious and immutable laws. Despite the destruction of forty-eight synagogues during the twenty-year period from 1948 to 1967, the old Jewish quarter was rebuilt after 1967, immediately following the reunification, almost identical to its former self. To be sure, when I say "identical," you have to take into account the technical advances of the modern era: the new buildings are infinitely more spacious, more airy, and more salubrious than those they replaced, where dust and obscurity often fought for supremacy. But the new synagogues were rebuilt on the ruins of those blown up by Glubb Pasha's

Arab Legion, which virtually leveled them. Only a few of the original buildings still stand, such as the entrance arch of the Hurva Synagogue, which was constructed in 1856 thanks to a generous gift of the Emperor Franz-Joseph I, whom the Galician Jews referred to affectionately by "Judaizing" his name to Franz-Yossef.

The old Jewish quarter that I visited as an adolescent is once again there, cheek-by-jowl with the Armenian quarter, and descending the steep streets toward the Western Wall, commonly but incorrectly known as the Wailing Wall.

Never since the time of the Second Temple has that spot been the focus of so much attention. Up until 1948, to get there visitors had to make their way through a series of narrow, filthy streets, whose inhabitants watched with undisguised hostility the crowd of Jewish pilgrims hurrying toward the last remaining vestige of Israel's ancient splendor. A narrow passageway no more than thirty feet wide was cleared away below the esplanade of the Mosque so that the Jews, at carefully prescribed hours, could proceed with their prayers. And woe unto him who in any way transgressed these strict limits of time or space. From 1920 to 1947, the Hakotel Hamaaravi, the Western Wall, was the site of frequent murderous acts between Jews and Arabs, each faction convinced that its God — who was the only true God — and justice were on its side. From 1948 to 1967 Jews were forbidden from even going to the Kotel. Since the Six-Day War, the site has changed considerably. The narrow, thirty-foot area has been greatly expanded, replaced by a broad paved esplanade where thousands of the faithful gather on Friday evening and on feast days. Since 1967 Jews are no longer forbidden to worship at this strange site, which, for many long centuries, was the only place on earth they could call home. For hundreds of years, millions and millions of men and women from all around the world harbored the hope that they might once again come and pray at the foot of this wall. This fervor is doubtless the basis of the custom whereby pilgrims today slip into the interstices of the stones humble messages, often written in unsteady script, beseeching the happiness of good fortune for their families and their people, a custom still very much in vogue today, even among those who are not religious.

From his *Diary,* I knew Herzl would be irritated and upset by the omnipresence of panhandlers and certain Hebrew-speaking religious predators who sell their services to their brethren who do not know the language. In his entry for October 31, 1898, he notes:

> We have been to the Wailing Wall. Any deep emotion is rendered impossible by the hideous, miserable, scrambling beggary pervading the place. At least such was the case, yesterday evening and this morning, when we were there.

Nevertheless, I still planned to take him there. I am the first to be painfully aware of these imperfections, these assaults on the dignity of the place, but these are mere trivialities when compared to what one feels in the depths of one's heart in the presence of this miraculously surviving portion of the Temple of Jerusalem. And I love the legend that the Western Wall was the only one saved from destruction because it was built by the poor of Jerusalem, those who throughout Jewish history somehow stubbornly managed to remain faithful to their ancestral beliefs.

I suggested to Herzl that we spend one entire day at the Wall, to show him that the faithful are here around the clock, for it is at this place that the Shekhinah (the divine presence) wanders, seeking consolation through the prayers of the children of Israel for the evils that have beset Jerusalem through the ages, and still do today.

This spot is both a place of memory and an incredible incentive to tolerance and universalism. Within the stones of the Wall reside the hopes — past, present, and future — of the Jewish people. To say the Wall inspires tolerance and universalism may seem surprising, for so many religions claim to have a monopoly on this tiny piece of earth. And yet it is only when I meditate before the Wall that I understand fully what Christians and Muslims alike must feel in the presence of their most holy places, the Church of the Holy Sepulcher and the esplanade of the Mosque. I know no more privileged moment than those brief instants of grace when the chant of the Jewish faithful mingles with the muezzin's call to prayers and the sound of the bells of the various churches of the City of David. Herzl and I witnessed such a communion, and it showed my companion that the description of the Old

City in *Old-New Land* was not solely the product of his imagination. In any event, here, where my own roots lie, other roots are growing that represent other forms of man's aspiration for peace and a higher realm of thought. May the reader forgive me for speaking only of the Wall, and not of the Church of the Holy Sepulcher or the El Aksa Mosque; it is simply that, no matter how much one respects other religions, one speaks in a more informed way by focusing on what one knows personally.

I didn't want to spend too much time with Herzl focusing on religion. In Jerusalem, more than anywhere else in the world, religion (or, more exactly, a false interpretation of religion) creates invisible barriers between people — between Jews and non-Jews, between Christians and Muslims, between Jews and Jews, between Christians and Christians. During our stay in Jerusalem, I explained to him that these barriers not only divide communities one from the other but also tend to create borders between the various sects and groups whose followers, often of the same religion, are ready to die for their beliefs. The American writer Saul Bellow, who visited Jerusalem a number of years ago, tells the following story that illustrates the problem. One day when he was strolling in the vicinity of the Church of the Holy Sepulcher, he climbed a steep, narrow street, at the top of which he came upon a door ajar, somewhere halfway between heaven and earth. Pushing it open, he found himself literally under the eaves of the church, where some servants of God were living. Intrigued, Bellow asked one of the men how they had come to live in such an odd spot. The man explained that he was a member of the little Ethiopian sect that possessed certain traditional rights to the Church of the Holy Sepulcher. Bellow asked his Israeli guide why these people had sought refuge in the church rafters.

"About a hundred and ten years ago," the guide responded, "the Coptic rivals of this sect somehow managed to change the locks of the church's main doors, as a result of which the Ethiopians were locked out and took refuge behind this green door, so as to remain faithful to their given mission. And so things remained for a hundred years. It wasn't until the Six-Day War that the Egyptians were able to install new locks on the church doors and regain their ancient rights."

This in no way eliminated, or even lessened, the hostility of the Copts who had perpetuated the "crime" to start. In Jerusalem, the person in charge of hearing and hopefully resolving such disputes — a post traditionally held by a pious Jew — inevitably sees a steady stream of complaints land on his desk day in and day out: Catholic against Orthodox, Orthodox against Protestant, Protestant against Copt and Nestorian, these last generally in connection with some presumed infraction on the part of one or the other relative to the celebration of their services at the Church of the Holy Sepulcher. If nothing else, this situation has the virtue of demonstrating that Jews do not have a monopoly on this kind of operatic shenanigans, even though it is an area in which they are known to excel.

Although Herzl took a fairly dim view of Jerusalem a hundred years ago, I'm afraid that, by describing the city today as even more divided than it appears at first glance — reflecting the propensity on the part of the inhabitants to revel in discord — I gave him even greater reason to despair of human folly. As we strolled through the Mea Shearim quarter of the city, it fell to me to explain that at the far end of the Street of the Prophets lay the invisible frontier between Jewish Jerusalem and Arab Jerusalem. I went on to explain that the other end of that same street marks the invisible frontier between the ultra-orthodox Jews of the city and the secular Jews, two entirely different worlds that seem not to be living under the same skies or in the same geographical area, despite sharing the same city and the same calendar. To further illustrate the immense complexity and contradictory nature of the city, I tried to explain to him that Jerusalem could embrace two such different and disparate people as Gershom Scholem, an agnostic historian, and an ultra-religious shoemaker of Mea Shearim.

"What's so earthshaking about that?" Herzl asked.

"Gershom Scholem, who was a bit of an anarchist, was also a renowned scholar on the subject of Jewish mysticism," I said, "while the shoemaker, a member of the Orthodox and anti-Zionist group Neturei Karta — the Guardians of the City — was also one of the world's foremost specialists on none other than Friedrich Nietzsche, and recognized as such."

Herzl looked at me askance. I had the feeling he was

asking himself if he wasn't dealing with a bunch of lu-
natics who claimed to be his disciples. He was probably
telling himself that this country has a very strange and
devastating effect on those who live here! The deep fur-
row on his brow made me fear he was going to lose his
temper and threaten to cut short our journey. This in turn
reminded me of the epitaph he had wanted engraved on
his tomb: WE HELD THE JEWS IN TOO HIGH ESTEEM.

I decided to change the subject and drew his attention to one of contemporary Jerusalem's most distinctive
features, namely the predominance of ocher in its buildings, be they new or old, a rather pleasant legacy from the
city's most recent occupants, the English, who were the
last in a long line of occupiers over the centuries. Ronald
Storr, the British military governor of Jerusalem, man-
dated that all new houses constructed in Jerusalem be
built of smoothly hewn stone, or at least have the façades
of their walls made of stone. That appeared to calm Herzl
down, and I suggested we take a short trip to Gershon-
Agron Street, near the Mamilla Wall — not far from where
he had stayed in 1898 — to visit the most surrealistic museum on earth. I was not referring to the splendid Israel
Museum across from the Knesset, which houses, among
other treasures, the Dead Sea Scrolls, but to the modest
Taxation Museum, which occupies the entire ground floor
of a building on that street. This museum is the repository
of various historical documents relating to the taxes,
levies, penalties, and assessments that Jews were obliged

to pay, no matter who the occupying powers were over the centuries. And when you take into account that today's Israeli taxpayer has one of the highest rates on earth, you can readily understand why I call this museum "surrealist."

No matter what my companion's frame of mind at this juncture, we could not leave Jerusalem without visiting a terrible but essential site, located not far from the hill that bears his name. Down the road from Mount Herzl is the Yad VaShem memorial, built to commemorate the six million victims of the Shoah, that "final solution to the Jewish problem" decreed by Adolf Hitler.

To be sure, the Passover Haggadah teaches us that in "each and every generation someone emerges to exterminate us." But Hitler's pogrom far exceeded all previous pogroms visited upon the Jewish people throughout their long history. This time there was no way out: converting to Christianity or to some other religion was not an option. The order was all-encompassing: all Jews, converted or not, believers or nonbelievers, Zionists or anti-Zionists, men, women, and children, old people and babes-in-arms, were to be erased from the face of the earth. And all that occurred only a little more than half a century ago, in the heart of a Europe that prided itself on being the cornerstone of modern civilization. Further — and this was the hardest part for Herzl to grasp — this crime against humanity was committed by the Germans, although aided and abetted by the citizens of a number of other nations, to be sure. These were the same Germans whose language and culture Herzl, and so many other Jews of his time, not only held dear but truly venerated.

Although he was sadly convinced that there was no way of plucking out the demon of anti-Semitism from the hearts and minds of non-Jews, the author of *Old-New Land* was astounded and overwhelmed that *rishess* — the Yiddish term for Judeophobia — could go so far as to call for the systematic extermination of his people. In *The Jewish State*, he had viewed Zionism as the only way for the Jews to escape their condition as isolated minorities or as third-class citizens of history, a millennia-long situation that neither emancipation nor any other internal solution could remedy.

> We have honestly endeavored everywhere to merge ourselves in the social life of surrounding communities and to preserve the faith of our fathers. We are not permitted to do so. In vain are we loyal patriots, our loyalty in some places running to extremes; in vain do we make the same sacrifices of life and property as our fellow-citizens; in vain do we strive to increase the fame of our native land in science and art, or her wealth by trade and commerce. In countries where we have lived for centuries we are still cried down as strangers, and often by those whose ancestors were not yet domiciled in the land where Jews had already had experience of suffering. The majority may decide which are the strangers. . . . If we could only be left in peace. . . .
>
> But I think we shall not be left in peace.

Neither Herzl, nor those who succeeded him in the Zionist movement, could ever have foreseen that people's inability to "leave the Jews in peace" would take the shape of such a concerted and radical effort to wipe out the entire race. Herzl, a great admirer of Heinrich Heine, had not paid sufficient heed to the great German poet's prescient words of warning — even though Friedrich, the hero of *Old-New Land*, remembers fondly Heine's *Hebraic Melodies* as he goes to the temple on Friday evenings. Despite his light, ironic touch, and however great his personal charm, Heine was no fool, and his mind was razor sharp. He belonged to the long race of prophets, as this extraordinary passage from his book *On Germany* so clearly demonstrates:

> Christianity, and this is its finest achievement, quietened this brutal Germanic lust for battle to some degree, but could not eradicate it entirely, and if one day that subduing talisman, the cross, is broken, then the savagery of the ancient warriors will rattle its weapons afresh in the senseless rage of the Berserkers of which the Nordic poets tell in song and story. The talisman is rotten, and the day will come when it collapses lamentably; then the old stone gods will arise from the forgotten rubble, and Thor with his gigantic hammer will spring aloft and smash the Gothic cathedrals. . . . Do not laugh at my advice, the advice of a dreamer warning you against Kantians, Fichteans, and philosophers of nature. Do not laugh at the visionary who expects the same revolution to occur in the phenomenal realm as has happened in the realm of the mind. Thought precedes action as lightning precedes thunder. German

thunder, of course, being German, is not very agile, and rolls along rather slowly; but it will arrive in due course, and when you hear such a crash as has never yet been heard in the history of the world, then you will know that German thunder has finally reached its goal. When its sound is heard, the eagles will drop down dead from the sky, and the lions in the remotest deserts of Africa will draw in their tails and creep into their royal caves. A play will be performed in Germany, compared to which the French Revolution will seem a mere inoffensive idyll.

Unfortunately, this visionary text is far too little known, and I decided to read it in full to Herzl as we strolled along the paths of Yad VaShem, especially as we walked down the Avenue of the Righteous among the Nations, flanked by the trees planted in memory of all those non-Jews who risked their lives to save the Jews. During the rest of our visit to Yad VaShem, I pointedly refrained from any comment. I simply let the photographs and documents that fill the rooms of the museums speak for me. It is indeed appropriate that such a memorial be constructed in Jerusalem, the center of Jewish hope, a hope that transcends the most terrible dramas and tragedies. In a city of "ruin and desolation," it is good that a site exists to remind us constantly of when darkness and despair held Jewish history in a viselike grip.

*

* *

From Yad VaShem, you can see the valley of Ein Kerem and the hills of Judea, whose rounded flanks stretch toward the Dead Sea and the site of ancient Moab. And it is here I wanted to end my tour of Jerusalem with Theodor Herzl. Having paid our respects both to the Wailing Wall and to Yad VaShem, I took him to one of the other important places of Jewish history: Masada, the fortress built by King Herod the Great at the edge of the Dead Sea. There the survivors of the last great Jewish revolt, which took place from 66 to 73 C.E., under siege by the Roman legions encamped below — more than fifteen thousand strong — preferred to commit suicide rather than yield to servitude. In this majestic place whose very stones bear the weight of tragic history, the voice of Eliezer Ben-Yair rang out on the night of April 15 in the year 73 as he addressed his comrades-in-misfortune:

> We are born but to die; that is an inexorable law of Nature before which all men, however happy and healthy, are compelled to bow. But do not force us to suffer the outrages of servitude. Therefore, let us die together with those we hold most dear, rather than live as slaves.

Of the approximately one thousand Zealots within the fortress, 967 took their lives; only two women and five children survived.

There was a reason for taking Herzl to Masada directly following our visit to Yad VaShem. These two tragic sites are emblematic of a certain conception, which today is happily behind us, both of Zionism and of Israel itself. This is the so-called Masada complex: the notion prevalent among the early generations of Sabras, constantly under siege from without, that suicide is better than defeat. I intended to show Herzl that, several decades after the founding of our state and only a little more than a century after the Congress of Basel, we have rid ourselves of this complex and the notion that the state might one day disappear.

The defeatist attitude is disappearing, though it has had a profound effect upon four generations of Sabras, raised in the shadow of Masada and Yad VaShem. The emblematic figures of Eliezer Ben-Yair and Mordechaï Aniliewicz, the hero of its Warsaw ghetto, seemed to superimpose themselves upon the acts and attitudes of Israeli leaders every time a major political decision had to be made. Both the overriding fear of catastrophe, and the fascination with the notion of making a grand exit into History (perishing with honor in the midst of a hostile environment or opting for suicide rather than renouncing the notion of national independence) have ceased to hold sway as they once did. We have made peace treaties with the PLO as well as with a number of Arab states — all of which are proof positive that the state of Israel is here to stay.

Today, we know that if we truly desire a just and lasting peace when it comes to the Israeli-Palestinian situation, and if we are prepared to work toward that end as quickly and tenaciously as we can, we will no longer be threatened with annihilation.

We must always keep the memory and meaning of Masada and Yad VaShem alive in our hearts. I also believe we must instill in our people another hope, which I would symbolize by the Ein Gedi, the lush countryside not far from Masada, that miraculous spring in the desert that was near and dear to the hearts of both David and Solomon, Israel's two greatest kings. That wonderful spot, hidden in the hollow of the rocks, whose lush greenness contrasts so sharply with the aridity of the surrounding hills, represents life and the future. The very mention of it brings instantly to mind the words of the Sulamite in Song of Solomon:

> My beloved is to me a cluster of henna blossoms
> in the vineyards of En ge'di.
> (Song of Solomon 1:14)

I therefore took Herzl there. Going from Jerusalem to Ein Gedi, we passed another extraordinary site, Qumran, the site where the Dead Sea Scrolls were found just at the moment when the state of Israel itself was about to be born. I told Herzl that if we had made a side trip to Qumran, it would have been not solely because of the astonishing archaeological digs that took place there — and are still taking place today — but because in its own way Qumran symbolizes one of the countercurrents against which our people still have to struggle. At the beginning of the Christian era, Qumran was home to the Essenes, who, along with the Pharisees and Sadducees, were one of the principal Jewish sects of the time. To escape from what they viewed as the evil within the society of their day, the Essenes withdrew into the desert. There is a parallel to be drawn between the Essenes of two thousand years ago and a small minority of today's extreme-right Zionists, those who claim that colonizing the territories is the equivalent of *halutsiut,* the pioneer spirit of old. Upset either by the increasing secularism of the state and society or by a decline in overt nationalism, some of my compatriots claim to be following in the footsteps of the Essenes as they set up colonies outside the 1967 borders. This movement is a result of the growing sense most Israelis have that national identity is no longer a goal but a reality, and they are incapable of living in the rapidly evolving modern world, where most Israelis feel quite at home. They are not so much setting forth to conquer new territories as turning their backs on Israeli society — that society that Herzl so ardently desired and dreamed of, a society whose heart Herzl placed squarely in Haifa, the next stop on our voyage.

3

THE BAY OF HOPE

*W*hen the story of our voyage in Eretz Israel is duly recorded in history, it will be noted that it did not follow the rules of either logic or comfort. For our trip to Haifa, I suggested to my companion that rather than travel by bus or train, we revert to the coastal traffic that people once used but no longer do. We boarded a fishing boat at Jaffa to take us by sea the short distance to Haifa.

Before embarking, I very carefully made certain our little offshore expedition would not suffer any unforeseen unpleasant weather. Leaning nonchalantly against the handrail, we could feel the boat rock gently beneath us as we watched the villas of Herzliyya — the city named in his honor in 1924 by American Zionists — slip slowly past. A bit farther on we also had a chance to view, first the Roman ruins of Caesarea, then, a few miles farther north, the rich archaeological site of Tel Dor and the crusader castle of Athlit, before we turned into Haifa's majestic bay. We approached the shore without the slightest concern about barrier reefs, such as those that claimed so many souls off Jaffa. I was counting on the beauty of the landscape, dominated by the lofty peak of Mount Carmel, to attenuate Herzl's probable disappointment at the way Haifa has evolved over the years since his last visit. However undeniable the city's charm may be — and legend has it that it derives its name from the two Hebrew words *ha* and *yaffe* ("beautiful shore") — Herzl found it very different from the idyllic description he gave it in his utopian novel. He had written *Old-New Land* at a time when Tel Aviv had not yet risen out of the sands adjoining Jaffa, and decided that Haifa would become the great economic and commercial center of Jewish Palestine. It was at Haifa that the two heroes of his novel, Kingscourt the Christian and Loewenberg the Jew, disembarked upon their return to the Holy Land after so many years away.

Their excursion was in many ways not unlike ours: hastily improvised. Kingscourt and Loewenberg had had no intention of returning to a country they had already visited more than two decades before and found to be a place of desolation and indescribable poverty. But during their stopover in the port of Alexandria, they overheard officers and sailors alike singing the praises of Haifa, whose merits they extolled in great detail. Although they remained skeptical, our two voyagers decided to delay their return to Europe and see for themselves whether there was any truth to the stories or whether they were simply the tall tales that sailors tend to tell, especially after a few glasses too many. Kingscourt and Loewenberg were delighted they did, for what they saw when they arrived in Haifa — the episode was set in 1923 — dazzled them both. According to Herzl, Haifa had evolved into a major maritime port, compared to which both Suez and Alexandria cut a sorry figure. The modest yacht the novel's heroes leased was almost lost as it slipped in between the enormous cargo ships that lined the docks, unloading, with an infernal and incessant clanking of conveyor belts, cargo from all over the world. And there were huge passenger ships as well. As for the city itself, it had turned into a big, bustling European city such as one finds up and down the Mediterranean coast. On the flanks of Mount Carmel hundreds of private houses had been built, each with its own garden bursting with exotic blooms. You could easily believe you'd landed somewhere in France's Côte d'Azur or Spain's Costa Brava, not far from Nice or Barcelona. But a number of "slender minarets soaring straight into the morning light" reminded the visitors, who momentarily imagined they were in another, Western city, that they were indeed in the Middle East — a region that had at long last shaken off its age-old lethargy and gleamed brightly with a thousand fires.

When we arrived, therefore, I was more or less prepared for Herzl's less than lyric reaction to the city today.

"I'm surprised there aren't more ships in the port," he said, barely masking his disappointment. "And the few that are here are, how shall I say, rather modest in size."

"There's good reason for that," I responded. "Ours is the age of Icarus, and today it's far cheaper to carry not only cargo but people by air than by sea. Not to mention far faster."

While he had little trouble understanding how the rapid evolution of air traffic had radically changed the port of Haifa, I knew it would be far tougher for me to explain why today's Haifa did not contain the square to which he had given the rather grandiose name of Nation's Square. He had envisaged this grand and majestic square as flanked on all sides by buildings housing all the major European shipping companies. In the center would be a garden filled with palm trees planted in double rows, such as you find lining the major avenues of Mediterranean cities. We don't lack for palm trees in Haifa. The city is full of them, as is Tel Aviv and so many other Israeli cities, but the administration of public thoroughfares has not had the poetic vision to use them the way Herzl planned in *Old-New Land*. He had written, "They gave shade by day, and at night shed light from electric lamps which hung from them like enormous glass fruits." The town fathers, pragmatic above all, confined themselves to erecting simple streetlights, which are infinitely less poetic and ecologically sound than those Herzl had envisioned.

Nor was that my companion's only subject of discontent. As he watched the people passing by in the streets he remarked with a slight frown, "Where are all the Chinese and Persians I said would feel right at home here in this port, which I predicted would be the safest and most peaceful in the Mediterranean basin?"

I told him that there was a Japanese pavilion on the side of Mount Carmel, which housed a museum of Japanese art, but he was hardly appeased. I did my best not to acknowledge the disappointment I knew he was feeling, and remained stoically quiet when I saw him lift his eyes heavenward, as if he were looking for something there. I knew all too well what his eyes were searching for. Herzl greatly admired the work of Jules Verne, and had predicted that Haifa would one day be equipped with a kind of aerial railway, which would run above the rooftops, a series of coaches suspended from an overhead electrical line that would whisk passengers from one end of the city to the other. When I showed him the modest cable car that carries passengers up Mount Carmel, straining as it goes, he shook his head in disbelief. I was sure he was saying to himself, "No question, Jews will be Jews! Who else in the world would have the chutzpah to label this minuscule miniature train the 'Metro,' literally asking that it be compared to those impressive subterranean rail systems of New York, Paris, London, and Moscow?" No matter: the citizens of Haifa are rightfully proud of their "subway," as they are proud of their entire city.

Despite Herzl's clothes, which were roughly a century out of date, more than a few natives of Haifa recognized my companion and came up to him, as we descended from our boat. Showing little or no compunction, they introduced themselves and touted their city's multiple virtues. Knowing that he had already visited Tel Aviv and Jerusalem earlier in his voyage, both of whose inhabitants they assumed would have boasted about how modern their cities were, or how steeped in antiquity, the citizens of Haifa made a special point of explaining to Herzl that he should not believe a word of anything negative people might say about Haifa.

"Haifa," one said, "is both ancient *and* modern. Ancient because all sorts of archaeological digs have shown that Haifa itself, and the surrounding area, have been inhabited since the dawn of time. In fact, the karstic caves on the slopes of Mount Carmel were occupied by both *Homo sapiens* and his ancestor *Homo erectus* as far back as the Middle Paleolithic period."

Another, holding a Bible in his hand, opened it to various passages that attested to the fact that Haifa and its earliest inhabitants were cited therein. "The majesty of Carmel and Sharon," intoned the reader, citing Isaiah, "they shall see the glory of the Lord, the majesty of our God."

"Just look at Mount Carmel," a third denizen trumpeted, "it was there that the prophet Elijah challenged King Ahab. After his marriage to Jezebel, the daughter of the king of Tyre, Ahab had allowed various cults of idolatry to flourish in his kingdom, especially the cult of Baal."

Elijah, an emblematic figure of the revolt, gained the

established power in the name of a monotheistic ideal, and provoked and challenged the priests of Baal. In so doing, he brought down upon himself the mortal wrath of the king, from whom he miraculously escaped only by being swept up and taken to heaven by a whirlwind.

"If Jerusalem, with its Wall, was for centuries the heart and soul of Jewish hope," said another proud citizen of the city, "we could say the same about Elijah, and therefore about Mount Carmel and Haifa." This is quite true: tradition has it that it will be the return of Elijah that will announce the coming of the messianic era.

Herzl nodded in agreement, clearly impressed by the zeal and erudition of his young interlocutors, but before he could utter a word another member of the group chimed in.

"Just because Haifa is mentioned in the Bible," he said, "doesn't mean that our city isn't as young as Tel Aviv . . . or almost."

He went on to remind Herzl — in case he didn't know — that the place the Greeks called Zeus's promontory had been totally abandoned for centuries. The others then enumerated, with solemn faces, the vicissitudes of the city, which was reconstructed at the time of the Crusades, then destroyed in 1265 by the Mamluks. It wasn't until the nineteenth century that a governor of Acre had a small fort and a lighthouse — the Stella Maris (Star of the Sea) Lighthouse — built on the city's ruins not far from the grotto of the prophet Elijah.

So caught up were they in their discussion that I was

all but certain one of them would dash home and come back with one of those old tin boxes, either bought at an antique market or fetched down from the attic. It once would have held a now-defunct brand of coffee, "The Haifa Planter," a somewhat bizarre brand name given the fact that no coffee had ever been grown in the region. Be that as it may, the label on the box depicted the country-side around the bay of Haifa as completely bare — not even a house.

"This label was painted in the 1860s," said one young lady — who indeed had come back with the pretty relic — "which goes to show how young our city really is!"

A number of our newfound friends, taking Herzl's arrival among them as perfectly natural, made a point of complimenting him on his prescience when, in *Old-New Land*, he had had the wisdom and foresight to place his aerial Metro — the ultimate symbol of modernism — in their city. For it was the extraordinary and rapid evolution of the means of transportation in the nineteenth century that enabled Haifa to develop into an important center of communication, starting in 1880. It was in that year that a group of Russian and Rumanian Jews arrived to join the small North African Jewish community already established there in the *harat al-Yahad* — the Jewish quarter.

In 1912 the first stone was laid for what in 1954 would be called the Technion, the principal engineering school of the country. This was more or less the same period when Tel Aviv was rising from the dunes, which tends to show that in modern terms both cities are, as the natives of Haifa claimed, sisters, almost like twins. That also may explain the intense rivalry between the two cities. They are too much alike not to try and distinguish themselves from each other. Honesty obliges me to admit that modern Haifa did indeed evolve at more or less the same time as Tel Aviv. Both cities benefited from the massive waves of immigration after World War I. In the brief span of twenty-two years, from 1922 to 1944, the two key dates when the British authorities took a census, the number of Jewish inhabitants of Haifa increased more than tenfold, going from six thousand to sixty-six thousand. Among them were many refugees from Hitler's Germany, including the writer Arnold Zweig, then world famous though scarcely remembered today. His correspondence with Sigmund Freud recounts the different, and often difficult, stages of Jewish Haifa's resurrection. Living conditions in that industrious city were often far less wonderful than the glorious countryside all around might lead you to believe, and many of the newcomers had a hard time adjusting to their new life. High on the list of problems was the lack of heat during the winter months, as a letter from Zweig to Freud, dated January 1934, amply demonstrates:

> You are going to think, dear Papa Freud, that I am dwelling far too long on this problem of central heating, but these practical matters, when indeed these appliances of civilization work only partially and painfully, remain at the core of the country's problems. We are not ready to give up our level of comfort, and this country is not yet in a position to satisfy it. And since the Palestinian Jews are rightly

proud of what already exists, and we are just as rightly irritated by what does not, the frictions between are numerous.

That letter is more symbolic than anything else. It matters little that both the author and the recipient were
world-renowned personalities. What does matter is that in
the light of a minor problem such as the one mentioned
by Zweig, we have a chance to measure the degree to
which Israel, in the intervening six and a half decades, has
tried — with considerable success in my view — to
bridge the gap between "what already exists" and "what
does not." We have indeed made tremendous strides in
that direction.

Were Zweig to join Herzl and me in Haifa today, I'm
sure he would be the first to agree. But his letter of 1934
remains an eloquent testimony to the prevailing mentali-
ties of the time. At about this same period, Chaim Weizmann, the future president of Israel, who was fully aware
of the difficulty German Jews were having integrating
into their new climate, said at the occasion of the first
Zionist congress, "God only knows how that poor little
Land of Israel is going to absorb this veritable flood of immigrants and come out of it with a healthy social structure."

Like Tel Aviv, Haifa is proof positive that arguments
on both sides — from both newcomers and the established — were unjustified. Haifa's Jewish quarters, built
around its Arab neighborhood, could be compared to the

way Tel Aviv was built around Jaffa: a new agglomeration, constructed with love, by the generation of builders, which was also that of the founders.

I remarked to Herzl that present-day Haifa has nothing to be ashamed of compared to his utopian description of it in *Old-New Land*. Moreover, he was right on target when he made Haifa the center of maritime commerce in the eastern Mediterranean. That was the very role it played at the beginning of World War II, when Beirut and the Syrian ports were under Vichy's control. The oil pipeline from Iraq ended at the foot of Mount Carmel, where some of the crude was refined. And it was through Haifa that the combined British, Free French, and Polish forces under the control of General Anders were able to pass, thus preventing Syria and Lebanon, both of which were under French control, from falling into the hands of the Germans, which could well have had incalculable consequences for the outcome of the war.

Since 1948, the pipeline has unfortunately ceased to function, because our neighbors have decreed it so. But one can easily foresee how, once there is a peace agreement between Israel and Syria, it could be reopened, which would be of enormous benefit to both the city and the region. That is but one of the countless benefits I envision — and hope for with all my heart — from the eventual creation of a Common Market in the Middle East. Haifa, like Tel Aviv, will be a door opening onto the future, a young city, a *very* young city, whose real history still lies before it. In its own way, Haifa's high-tech industries, which can compare to the best Silicon Valley has to offer, already prove that point, and lend further credibility to Herzl's dream. I told him as much, and I could see from the slight smile on his face and twinkle in his eyes that I had hit home.

During the rest of our stay, Herzl was pleased, absolutely fascinated, by the astonishing complexity of Haifa, which is half European and half Mideastern, half Jewish and half Arab, half secular and half religious, half classic and half ultramodern, as if incapable of choosing among its various aspects for fear of losing one or more and thus losing some of its cachet.

*

* *

The small group of Haifa natives who had met us at the boat and touted the many and varied virtues of their fair city wanted to take us on a grand tour. Our first stop was the imposing Dagon Grain Silo, one of the biggest and most beautiful in the world. Soaring over two hundred feet into the air, with a capacity of one hundred thousand tons, the silo is an eloquent reminder of how important the port of Haifa once was as a center for grain traffic. Our next stop was Wadi Nisnas, one of the Arab quarters of the city, whose narrow, winding streets are flanked by old stone houses with their grilled windows and vaulted doors. After the 1948 war, many Arabs chose not to flee, and today, I pointed out to Herzl, more than 10 percent of the city's population is made up of Druzes and Israeli Arabs, Christian or Muslim. At one of the restaurants on St. John Street we were invited in for a coffee or orange juice, but our impatient guides were anxious for us to visit two very different sites: the old city, which is infinitely less interesting than that of Jerusalem, and the industrial zone, which is key to Haifa's economic health. Then, turning our backs to the sea, we began our ascent of Mount Carmel, dotted with an eclectic mixture of old houses and ultramodern buildings, parks, museums, temples, and churches. The ample shade trees lend an air of peace to the slope, as do the brightly colored gardens of the sumptuous homes and mansions.

Used as he was to Vienna's parks, Herzl felt right at home here, where the sacred and secular sit side by side. Elijah's mountain is above all a mecca of spirituality. The world headquarters of the Carmelite order is here, as is the Baha'i Shrine, with its dome of twelve thousand gold tiles. Set in the midst of the sumptuous Persian Gardens, it is without doubt Haifa's most beautiful building. The shrine houses the remains of the founder of that religion, the Bāb (meaning "the Gate"), whose full name was Mirzā Alī Mohammed. In the mid-nineteenth century, this Muslim of Persian origin preached a new, universal message, offering a syncretist view of the world in which brotherhood, love, and charity are joined to the notion that all monotheistic religions are basically the same; only in their dogma do they differ. Thus the Bāb viewed Bābism as a normal progression of earlier monotheistic faiths. Persecuted in his native Persia, the Bāb was arrested and martyred in Tabriz, upon order of the Shah, in 1850. At the time of his death, Bābism counted some twenty thousand adherents. For more than half a century his followers kept his remains hidden. In the early years of the twentieth century, they purchased this plot of land on Mount Carmel as a suitably majestic place for his permanent burial.

The Bāb did not proclaim himself the messiah but the herald of such a one who would be called Bahā'Allāh. Thirteen years later, Bahā'Allāh announced that he was the Promised One foretold by the Bāb, and renamed the faith Baha'i. For all intents and purposes, the two faiths are one and the same.

The Baha'i movement enjoyed a spectacular growth over the century and a half since his death, and today counts roughly four million adherents worldwide.

"What made the Bāb's followers choose Haifa?" Herzl asked.

"Some people say quite by chance," I replied, "but I believe it was because Bahā'Allāh was kept under house arrest in Acre by the Ottoman authorities. He lived there until 1892, and after his death his son, taking advantage of the climate of tolerance under the British mandate, established the International Baha'i Center on Mount Carmel in the 1930s. . . ."

". . . of which the shrine, which I must say is stunning, is the crowning achievement," Herzl finished.

"After 1948," I went on, "the new Jewish state committed to honor the Baha'i Center. There are some three thousand Baha'i faithful who live here in Haifa today, alongside Jews, Christians, and Muslims."

"In peace and harmony," I thought I heard Herzl murmur. I couldn't tell whether it was a question or a comment. Assuming it was the former, I assented, "Yes, in peace and harmony. Unfortunately, I can't say the same for Jerusalem."

I thought Herzl would also be interested to learn that, because of that peaceful coexistence in Haifa, the city also is subject to a special statute concerning the Sabbath, which was instituted under the British mandate and still applied today: in contrast to the other cities of Israel, buses in Haifa run all day Saturday, except in certain areas, and theaters, movie houses, restaurants, and discotheques remain open on the Sabbath, unless the owners chose to close for their own religious reasons. All of which makes the city a lively place seven days a week.

The creaking cable car on Mount Carmel is not the only unusual "monument" there. Within the university stands the Levi Eshkol Tower, designed by Oskar Niemeyer, the architect both of the UN building in New York and the modern city Brasilia. From its observatory atop the thirty-story tower one has a splendid view of the entire north of the country — from the bay of Acre to the hills of Galilee, from the white cliffs of Rosh Ha-Nigra to the Golan Heights, and even, on a clear day, the snowy peaks of Mount Hermon and the Lebanese coast.

"Who was Levi Eshkol?" Herzl inquired.

It took some time to fill him in on the Six-Day War, which made this man of peace wince with despair.

During that key period, Levi Eshkol was prime minister, and though his name is inextricably linked with that time of conflict, he was in fact a peace-loving man known for his spirit of conciliation and willingness to compromise. In fact, some used to joke that so prone to compromise was he, so anxious not to ruffle feathers, that when his wife would ask him whether he wanted tea or coffee, he would respond, "Half tea, half coffee," a remark that has become legendary in Israel. It also explains why his name is affiliated with a profoundly cosmopolitan city, where compromise is an act of daily life and the key to peaceful coexistence among all segments of the population.

On his visit to Israel a century before, Herzl did not have a chance to visit the northern part of the country, though that had not prevented him from imagining, as he does in *Old-New Land*, what human labor and ingenuity could make of the coastal plain and hills of Galilee — that Galilee where the Zionist pioneers raised their voices in song, "El nivneh haGalil" ("We shall rebuild Galilee").

To end our visit to Haifa, I asked Herzl whether he would like to go to the top of Eshkol Tower, adding, out of deference, that I would understand if he were too tired. His withering look was my answer; of course he would go up to gaze upon the land that, as his hero David Littwak described it, was rich with fields and orchards and vineyards, reminding him of the French Riviera.

From the top of the tower he surveyed the scene with obvious pleasure, remarking on how close Littwak's vision was to reality. It was through this lush landscape that his protagonist had traveled on his way to Tiberias to celebrate Passover. Recollecting his many visits to the region of southern France around Nice and Cannes, and calling to mind the fragrant garigue that covers the hills around Grasse, Herzl transported them, with modification of course, to the Israel of his dreams: an enchanted valley inhabited by Russian Christian peasants who lived in complete harmony with their Jewish neighbors.

Herzl gazed across these northern hills and valleys, thinking, I was sure, "My dream has come true."

Still, Herzl had no idea just how this flowering of the desert came about. For that, a short trip to the village of Zippori, located between Haifa and Tiberias, was in order, to visit the moshav, or semicollective farm, there. The place is not without its charm, though in all fairness it does not have the majesty of Herzl's dream. But Zippori proved an appropriate place to discuss with Herzl the singular resurrection of the Land of Israel in modern times: to explain how the marshes were dried up, and how the deserts were turned into lush farmlands and orchards, thanks to a complex network of irrigation constructed by the pioneers who came here from the four corners of the world.

*

*   *

To many people, Israel is the country that caused the desert to bloom. Even though the Holy Land was not exactly the Sahara when the first Zionist immigrants arrived, these early settlers did turn the country into a place where milk and honey once again flowed, where agriculture thrived in the new context of the kibbutzim and moshavim. It took both me and the inhabitants of Zippori long hours to explain to Herzl exactly how all this came about. We started by reminding him that at the time Europe was already several decades into the industrial revolution, the Jews dreamed of nothing other than returning to the land, of becoming peasants and, later on, once they had conquered the land, researchers and scholars. It was necessary to get the milk and honey flowing first, after which technology would become the region's priority.

As a staunch proponent of the Enlightenment and technical progress, Herzl was profoundly convinced that the cities were the wave of the future. The fact that for centuries Jews had been forbidden by law to possess farmlands, and therefore were relegated to urban centers, gave them an advantage they could use in the future.

He had no intention of allowing them to give up this advantage. In *The Jewish State* he proclaimed to all who would hear his hostility to any attempt to send his fellow Jews back to the land. In Argentina, Baron Hirsch had made an unsuccessful attempt to create Jewish agricultural colonies, which Herzl roundly attacked: "Whoever would attempt to convert the Jew into a husbandman would be making an extraordinary mistake." With rare foresight, in which he rightly predicted the evolution of various European economies, he came to this drastic (but correct) conclusion. "The peasant," he wrote, "is . . . a type which is in course of extinction. Wherever he is artificially preserved, it is done on account of the political interests which he is intended to serve." And, even more presciently, he wrote, "The agrarian question is only a question of machinery. America must conquer Europe, in the same way as large landed possessions absorb small ones."

His predictions were all the more daring if one remembers that they flew in the face of the deeply rooted desires of most early Zionist pioneers, who dreamed of becoming peasants, of working, as soon as they were off the boat, the land that had been abandoned for centuries.

I confessed to my traveling companion that that was my dream, too, when I was young. In my Vichneva shtetl, the orchards around Tel Aviv represented the Israel in which I hoped one day to settle. And once I was there, I did become a modest actor in that agrarian movement. To pursue my secondary education, I left Tel Aviv behind and became a boarding student at the Ben Shemen Agricultural School, halfway between the coast and Jerusalem.

"I can tell you," I said to Herzl, anticipating a scornful laugh at the admission, "our attachment to the pastoral life was close to fanatic. To rebuild the Jewish homeland meant doing everything from milking cows to sharpening scythes, two activities at which I excelled in those days but would be hard pressed to try my hand at today."

But far from laughing, Herzl looked at me with what I took to be a glimmer of admiration, which encouraged me to go on.

"I was so committed, and so ideologically impassioned then, that my method of courting Sonia, who was later to become my wife, was to read her pages of Marx's *Das Kapital* and comment on them."

At this point, I noted, Herzl was smiling as he envisioned my youthful courtship.

"In retrospect, I only partially regret my heavy-handed tactic. Actually, I might even patent it, for I'm inclined to believe that therein lies the real usefulness of that weighty time: if your beloved can endure your reading Marx to her, that perhaps is the ultimate proof that she really loves you!"

"Where did you go after Ben Shemen?" Herzl wanted to know. I was flattered by his interest.

"I and several other boarding students were sent to the Gueva Kibbutz, in the sumptuous Jezreel Valley," I replied.

"Ah, yes," Herzl murmured, and I remembered that he had written about Jezreel a century earlier.

"The people at the Gueva Kibbutz were followers of A. D. Gordon, who championed the Jews' return to the land."

Feeling that Herzl really was interested in my early agrarian career, I barreled on. "After Gueva, I was sent to the Alumot Kibbutz, not far from Poryia, a place that offers a stunning view of the Lake of Tiberias."

"I'm sure you were a dedicated and excellent young farmhand," Herzl said paternally, but without a trace of condescension.

"In some ways, yes," I said. "But despite the wonderful view, I had my share of trials and tribulations at Alumot. At one point I was appointed shepherd of the kibbutz's flock of sheep. My job was to take the sheep from the kibbutz to the neighboring fields to graze, which proved no problem, sheep being docile. But then I was assigned to herd the kibbutz's cows to pasture, and that was a whole other story. The cows were a local breed known as Damas, endowed with a considerable sense of freedom. These highly undisciplined creatures did their damnedest to flaunt their independence, especially during the summer when they were irritated by swarms of flies or mosquitoes attacking them from all sides."

I had a feeling that Herzl, standing there stiffly in his dark, well-tailored suit, had to be trembling at the very thought of such a nonbucolic scene.

"Anyway, I spent most of my day trying to keep my cows from wandering away, running back and forth from one end of the field to another. I was a Jewish cowboy, but without a horse, and by the end of the day, dead with fatigue, I confess I had very mixed feelings not only about my Damas charges but also about the whole idea of sending Jews back to the land."

Herzl shook his head gravely, as though my personal tale had proved his point.

"It was that early experience in pragmatism," I said,

"that also showed me the reality does not always conform to the demands of ideology.

"Despite my reservations, the kibbutzim contributed mightily to the agricultural renaissance of the land of Israel. Together with the later reinforcement from the moshavim, they were responsible for the extraordinary development of our agriculture, whose products are today sold round the world. The vast majority of immigrants to Israel over the past several decades have opted to settle in the urban centers, but those hardy souls who did not contributed to the rebirth of a Jewish peasantry. True, like life itself, numerous changes are taking place in the management and duties of the kibbutzim. Yet they still play a very large role in the life of our state."

"When you say that," Herzl interrupted, apparently having read my mind, "I assume you're referring to the impressive number of exkibbutniks, men and women alike, who today also hold key positions in politics and the military."

I realized how much, and how quickly, the founder of Zionism had absorbed since his arrival, far more than I had imagined. But of course he was no ordinary visitor.

"Yes, of course, I was thinking of them," I said. "But I was also thinking of something else."

Herzl, I knew, could not be up to date on the rapid revolution of technology over the past century. But even when I gave him a quick rundown in this area, he was still surprised that so many exkibbutniks, so many Israelis who literally came from the farm, would later move into high technology. In my own small way I was involved, however peripherally, in one such technological development. As my fellow citizens doubtless remember all too well, not all that many years ago, if you wanted to make a phone call from a pay phone, you had to arm yourself with a pocketful of tokens, which, as I remember, the phones devoured voraciously, especially if the call wasn't local. And often the public phones were out of order, or vandalized, probably in most cases by people trying to coax those obnoxious but valuable tokens back from the machines.

During several trips I made to Paris in the early 1970s, I noticed that Parisians were using a magnetic card instead of tokens to gain entrance to the Metro. At that time I was minister of transportation and telecommunications, and when I got back to Israel after that Paris trip, I wrote to my French counterpart and asked him whether in his view that magnetic card might have any practical application in the realm of telecommunications. At the same time I asked him what company in what country manufactured the magnetic cards used in the Paris subway.

Much to my surprise, his reply, which was not long in coming, gave the address of the supplier of the Metro's magnetic card as the Gueva Kibbutz, the very place where I had learned to milk cows and sharpen scythes! Without ever renouncing its agricultural pursuits, the kibbutz had gotten deeply involved in high technology, and I had not had the slightest knowledge of it, nor even suspected that we had the capacity to produce such a sophisticated new "toy." We all know the old adage that says, "No one is a prophet in his own country," but this example brought home the truth of the saying.

"So you see," I concluded for Herzl's benefit, "we may not have built your aerial metro in Haifa, but we did make an important contribution toward improving the Paris Metro."

*

* *

That story gave us the excuse to direct our steps to the Gueva Kibbutz in the Jezreel valley, the resurrection of which has been made possible by the use of hydraulic resources and the perfection of a system of irrigation completely controlled by computers. Herzl was delighted at the idea of seeing this system work. He had long been fascinated by the question of water, which he considered one of the Middle East's most important commodities. I knew, too, that in this leg of our voyage, to Gueva and Lake Tiberias, Herzl would be following in the footsteps of his protagonists of *Old-New Land*. In the course of that 1923 trip, David Littwak told his companions that the true creators of the future Land of Israel "were the hydraulic engineers. There was everything in having the swamps drained, the arid tracts irrigated, and a system of power supply installed," he wrote.

That passage shows again what a visionary Herzl was, and we need to think long and hard about both his predictions and his concerns as we approach the new millennium. While control of the water supply is key to continued economic growth in our region, it can also become the source of endless conflicts if we fail to handle it in a rational way. If we do fail, we will continue along the same dangerous path we are on today, namely the loss of half our national resources. Political and strategic consideration take precedence over human needs.

Humankind has made little or no progress from the time when nomad tribes battled over the ownership of a water source. Today in the Middle East, water is a precious commodity, infinitely more precious than the commodity known as black gold — oil. The relative lack of rainfall, plus the massive overutilization of our ground water by all the countries of the region, pose the very real risk of leaving us literally high and dry if nothing is done to correct the situation.

This is a problem we Israelis take very seriously. What would the Sea of Galilee* be without the incoming currents of the Jordan River and without the hidden sources on the ground of the lake, whose water level unfortunately continues to drop? The same is true of the Dead Sea, so much so that for a long time people seriously thought of digging a canal linking that body of water and the Mediterranean. In addition to setting up the desalination plants, we badly need to preserve the important

---

* This sea/lake is known under three names: The Kinneret, Lake Tiberias, and the Sea of Galilee.

reservoir constituted from the headwaters of the Jordan River and the other rivers in the north of the country, as we need to preserve all those other water sources in Israel, Lebanon, and Jordan. In 1955, the United States made a proposal to this effect to the various countries concerned, to no avail. The historical timing was simply not right, but today it is, certainly as regards a possible dialogue between Israel and Jordan. And I expect — or at least hope — the same will be true of Syria and Lebanon in the near future.

"I can assure you," I said to Herzl, "that this subject will be kept high on our list of priorities during peace negotiations with all these countries, as it is today in our discussions with the Palestinians concerning the water table of the Jordan hills.

"If we come to an agreement with the Palestinians on this point, it will set an example for all the other countries of the region. Both Iraq and Syria, for example, are worried about the effect the construction of the Atatürk Dam might have on the course of both the Tigris and Euphrates rivers."

I went on to explain, for I could see that Herzl was truly fascinated by this update of a subject near and dear to his heart, "Their worry of course is that Turkey might use this new dam to control the water flow, in other words use it as a geopolitical tool.

"I raised this question at great length some years back with the president of Turkey, Turgut Özal, an extremely intelligent man. I told him that in my view water was fully as much a commodity as oil, and that I could foresee the day when aquadollars would replace petrodollars on the world market. I also stressed that in my view Turkey could be blessed with a new era of prosperity if it could work out some general agreement with its neighbors concerning the equitable distribution of water, in the context of a regional common market. Jokingly, I said to him, 'Right now, fresh water is flowing into salt water, and the fish are paying you nothing. We Israelis are willing to pay.'"

"And then of course you have the age-old example of Egypt," Herzl opined. "Without the Nile . . ."

"Today," I added, "Egypt is even more acutely aware than ever how important it is to manage that 'gift of the Nile,' and how precarious it is as well. Its headwaters are located in no fewer than five countries: Zaire, Sudan, Uganda, Rwanda, and Ethiopia. Knowing how key the Nile is to its political and economic health, Egypt also is acutely aware that all five of these countries are or have recently been badly destabilized, which could have catastrophic water consequences for Egypt itself."

These two examples, Turkey and Egypt, suffice to show how correct Herzl had been to insist on the key importance of water resources for the Land of Israel. A trip to the north of the country gave us a chance to exchange views on the subject.

*

* *

I don't remember which wit said, with more than a trace of malice, "Israel's a nice place to visit in the morning. But what do you do in the afternoon?" How wrong he was. I've lived in this country since the early 1930s, and I often have the feeling I still have a great deal to discover. That is why I never wanted to limit this voyage to Tel Aviv, Jerusalem, Haifa, and Galilee. I wanted Herzl and me to visit every corner of the country, from the cliffs of Rosh Ha-Nigra to the Israeli-Lebanon frontier, to Elat on the Red Sea coast, and on to Ashdod, Ashkelon, Kyriat, Gat, Beersheba, Arad, Dimona, and a whole host of other places too numerous to mention.

Since we'd spent so much time on the subject of water, it seemed only fitting and proper to show Herzl the other side of the coin, and spend a week or so with him in the desert. I wanted to take him to the Negev, more specifically to Sde Boker, where David Ben-Gurion, my political and ideological mentor, lived out his final years. It was to this uncommon personage, born in a humble Jewish village in Poland, that befell the signal honor of both writing the Declaration of Independence of the state of Israel and reading it out loud to the people fifty-one years after the Congress of Basel, marking the realization of that wild dream nourished in a Parisian hotel room by a Viennese journalist.

I had a feeling these two men would have a great deal to discuss, and the desert would be a perfect place for them to meet. For in Israel, aridity, like water, is a source of life. That is what the old lion, with his white mane, affirmed in his own strange way. In a passage of his *Memoirs*, he evoked the arid landscape of Sde Boker in these words:

> The Negev offers the Jews their greatest opportunity to accomplish everything for themselves from the very beginning. This is a vital part of our redemption in Israel. For in the end, as man gains mastery over Nature he gains it also over himself. That is the sense, and not a mystical but a practical one, in which I define our redemption here.
>
> Israel must continue to earn its nationhood and to represent the Jewish people with their awesome past. It must be worthy of itself, which is no small achievement. It is one to be attained in the desert.
>
> When I look out of my window today and see a tree standing there, that tree gives me a greater sense of beauty and personal delight than all the vast forests I have seen in Switzerland or Scandinavia. Because every tree here was planted by us. It was nursed to life by the water we brought to it at such cost and effort. Why does a mother love her children? Because they are of her creation. Why does the Jew have affinity for Israel? Because here again everything remains to be accomplished. It is his privilege and his place to share in this creative act. The trees at Sde Boker speak to me in a special way, in another language than any other trees anywhere. Not only because I helped to grow them but because they constitute a gift of man to Nature, and a gift of the Jews to the cradle of their culture.

For Herzl as well as me, this stage of our journey was of great importance: we both needed the silent meditation in the desert solitude of Sde Boker to prepare us for the last stage of our journey. For now we were to meet the people of Israel in all their diversity. It would be a stage full of surprises and unforeseen events. Our moment of meditation in the desert helped prepare us for the reality that ensued — far different from what he had envisioned. For much more than the land, much more than the miracles wrought, the people, extraordinary and bewildering, represent the country's major, its prime, asset.

4

GENERATIONS

$\mathcal{E}$verything about today's Israelis took Herzl by surprise, beginning with their name — "Israelis." Herzl was a visionary genius about some matters but extraordinarily cautious about others, and one was assigning a name to the future inhabitants of the Jewish state. In *Old-New Land* he calls Israel the "New Society," a name everyone will agree is stunningly bland. I can just imagine today's customs officials examining a "New Society" passport and trying to figure out where on earth the bearer might be from.

David Ben-Gurion gave the new state being created the name "Israel" rather than the "New Society." "Israel" reminded the world that this new country was not being formed ex nihilo; it symbolized the renaissance of an ancient land that for so many centuries had lacked territorial identity. Calling the country "Israel" endowed it with a particular responsibility, for it is of course the name given to Jacob following his struggle with the mysterious "adversary" at the Yabbok crossing, "Your name shall no more be called Jacob, but Israel, for you have striven with God and with men, and have prevailed" (Genesis 32:28). Ours is the only country in the world whose very name constitutes both a challenge and a description of the human condition; above all it represents a Promethean struggle against greater forces, forces trying to deny it existence — but forces that can also overcome if the will can be summoned.

During his trip around Eretz Israel, Herzl had therefore not been meeting inhabitants of the "New Society"; he had been meeting Israelis. He had discovered they are a curious people, defying all logic. One of the thorniest questions in Israeli politics — and one which from time to time causes political crises — is, "What is a Jew?" One could also ask, "What is an Israeli?" "Israel" may be the name of the Jewish state, the realization of Herzl's dream, but not all Israelis are Jewish, nor are all Jews Israelis — far from it. Arab-Israeli delegates sit in the Knesset, representing a community that quite rightly believes itself to be part of Israel. These people are completely and absolutely Israeli. Moreover, a significant number of Jews who have been in Eretz Israel for some time are actively hostile to Zionism. They view assimilation into Israel as a form of sacrilege. "Why make things simple when you can make them complicated?" was purportedly the motto of the former Austro-Hungarian Empire; the same could be said of Israel.

*

* *

All this meant that as we walked together through the streets of Jaffa, Jerusalem, and Haifa, Herzl sometimes had difficulty guessing someone's ethnic origins. Is this or that person a European Jew, or from Maghreb, or the Middle East? Is he or she an Arab-Israeli, a Druze, or a Circassian? Things are even more complicated now that we all dress alike. In any event, Herzl now knew one thing: Israel contains more than a million non-Jewish citizens (out of a population of nearly 5 million), including 900,000 Muslims, 120,000 Christians of various origins, more than 70,000 Druzes, and 60,000 Bedouins. This is without even counting the several hundred Vietnamese boat people who have opened restaurants at which one can find the choicest Asian dishes, prepared according to Talmudic prescription.

That Israel is comprised of a mosaic of peoples and faiths delighted Theodor Herzl. Raised in the Hapsburg Empire — another formidable ethnic patchwork — he never confused nationalism with chauvinism. The New Society of which he dreamed was meant to be open to all. In *The Jewish State*, he proclaimed, "Every man will be as free and undisturbed in his faith or his disbelief as he is in his nationality. And if it should occur that men of other creeds and different nationalities come to live amongst us, we should accord them honorable protection and equality before the law." So deeply rooted was this belief that he refers to it again a year later, in a note in his *Diary* dated July 26, 1899. "My testament for the Jewish People: So build your State, that the stranger will feel contented among you."

For Herzl, the return of the Jews to the land of their ancestors did not mean banishing those already living in Eretz Israel. On the contrary, indigenous people were to be placed on an equal footing with the Jews; they were intended to be full-fledged members of the New Society, benefiting from the powerful social and economic changes wrought by Jewish immigration. This was why he created the character Reschid Bey in *Old-New Land*. Reschid is the prototype of the prosperous Arab, with a luxurious villa situated on the slopes of Mount Carmel. In the novel, Reschid Bey accompanies Kingscourt, Friedrich Loewenberg, and David Littwak on a trip to Tiberias, where they plan to celebrate Passover.

Convinced that Muslims get along better with the Jews than do Christians, Reschid is an eloquent proponent of the New Society. Asked about the consequence of the arrival of Jews into his land, his response is immediate, "It was a great blessing for all us. Naturally, the landowners gained most because they were able to sell to the Jewish society at high prices, or to wait for still higher ones. I, for my part, sold my land to our New Society because it was to my advantage to sell." Then Reschid begins to wax lyrical about how the two religions will be enriched by their contact.

To create Reschid Bey, Herzl did not rely purely on his imagination. Such a character existed in the person of Youssef Diya al-Khalidi, the former president of the municipal council of Jerusalem. In a letter he wrote in 1899 to Zadoc Kahn, the Great Rabbi of France (well known to Herzl), al-Khalidi called the idea of Zionism "natural, beautiful, and right," and looked forward to peaceful coexistence between Jews and Arabs.

Today it is popular to make fun of such naive proclamations, to see Herzl's vision of Arab-Jewish relations as paternalistic and condescending. It is said that we need to remember that these relations were far more antagonistic than the way Herzl portrayed them. Read late-nineteenth-century colonial literature, some say, and you will discover plenty of other examples of Europeans — soldiers, doctors, and missionaries — who believed that they represented the highest forms of civilization, and therefore looked upon the native inhabitants as primitives. Holier-than-thou colonial types were moreover not just rampant in Europe. They could also be found within the Zionist movement itself during the 1930s and 1940s.

When I was young I remember hearing my hard-core Marxist-Leninist schoolmates proclaiming they wanted to fight on the sides of their Arab brothers against British imperialism (even if these Arab brothers were not interested in their help). The true enemy, they maintained, were those members of bourgeoisie, whether Arab or Jewish, who trafficked with the British, and who were therefore responsible for giving rise to the hated "compradore" figure in the Middle East — the "Uncle Toms" who made concessions to the Europeans.

At the risk of shocking my former schoolmates (some of whom are still alive and may — though I think this unlikely — still cling to their early ideas), I myself prefer the thinking of Theodor Herzl and Reschid Bey. However naive and sentimental their pronouncements seem, they are more humane, more relevant, and more realistic than the dogmatic declarations of their detractors. Reflections on the nature of imperialism (does it or does it not represent the final stage of capitalism? et cetera) are of little use when it comes to formulating national policy. Militant Zionists must always remember the pluralist and multiethnic conception of the New Society that the author of *The Jewish State* wanted to realize in the land of his ancestors.

Indeed, to ensure that Israel remains a Jewish state, we must accept the existence of an adjacent Palestinian state. If we do not, Israel risks becoming binational — neither Jewish nor Palestinian — and condemned to chronic instability. The Palestinian question and the future of Israel, as Herzl had foreseen, are inseparable.

On at least one of these issues Herzl could with justification reproach us for not having heeded his advice. At the beginning of the century the Zionist movement was so preoccupied with creating a political and national identity for the Jewish people that it ignored the national aspirations of Arabs. Voices on both the Arab and the Jewish sides did try to make themselves heard on the issue. Neguib Azoury, the founder of the magazine *Carmel*, was less optimistic than Youssef Diya al-Khalidi. In 1905, in a pamphlet published in Paris (where *The Jewish State* was also published), Azoury noted:

> Two important phenomena of the same nature and yet opposites are taking shape today in Turkish Asia: the rise of the Arab nation and the effort by the Jews to reconstitute the ancient kingdom of Israel on a grand scale. These two movements are destined to be at war with each other until one or the other is victorious.

On the Jewish side, the brilliant humanitarian Ahad Haam, a proponent of a Zionism that was more spiritual than political in nature, warned his followers against neglecting the rights of the Arab population. He was picking up on something said by Herzl, though the two publicly disagreed with each other's positions. In this case, my companion would have agreed with what Ahad Haam had predicted:

> We need to rid ourselves of the illusion that Palestine is an empty country. We on the outside tend to imagine that the Arabs are savages of the desert, a stupid people with no distinguishing culture and no understanding of what is going on around them. This is a fundamental mistake. The Arabs understand very well what we are doing in this

country.... The day will come when the life of our people in the Land of Israel will expand to the point that it comes up against the local population. When that day comes, that population will not yield their land easily. We have to treat the local population with love and respect, in just and legal fashion. And yet what are our brothers in the Land of Israel doing? Precisely the opposite! As often happens when slaves becomes kings, they are treating the Arabs with hostility and cruelty, confiscating their property, striking them in shameful fashion, not only without cause but openly and proudly.

Herzl's successor, Chaim Weizmann, the former president of the Hebrew state and the man who negotiated with King Faisal II, the champion of Arab nationalism, shared Ahad Haam's point of view:

Most difficult is working with the Arabs who are, in fact, the inhabitants of the country. It is our duty to ease their fears, to convince them that there is room enough for all of us. It is our duty to explain that we want to work with them and that the establishment of the Jewish population will profit them.

*
*   *

We have paid a heavy price for our failure to reconcile the Jewish national movement and the nationalist aspirations of the Palestinian people. It would take several decades and the deaths of thousands before the voice of reason finally prevailed, and peace accords between our two peoples were signed. May they continue to find a path toward a long and fruitful collaboration, like the one wished for a century ago by Theodor Herzl and Youssef Diya al-Khalidi.

Whatever our failings, we Israelis have tried to create a multiethnic democratic society in which those of all religions can enjoy the same rule of law and live together in peace. That is what we mean by the "Israeli miracle" — and that is why we must oppose those for whom the realization of Jewish national aspirations is synonymous with a policy of exclusion. That kind of thinking leads to "ethnic purification" of the sort perpetrated in the former Yugoslavia.

I painfully and regretfully had to acknowledge to Herzl that during these last few years voices favoring the latter policy have been heard in Israel. We have seen the rise of groups and factions that revel in their minority status, and who would deny non-Jewish citizens fundamental rights — even call for their expulsion. The father of Zionism was the first to suspect that these hateful ideas, which run counter to Judaism's tradition of tolerance and sense of justice, might arise, and he denounced them with all his might.

In *Old-New Land*, Herzl embodied those who betray the spirit of Zionism by embracing messages of hate in the figure of a rabbi named Doctor Geyer, a proponent of expelling non-Jews from Israel. When they arrive in Neudorf ("new village"), a peaceful (and mythical) farming town, our heroes Littwak, Kingscourt, and Reschid Bey get into a heated argument with one of the town's inhabitants, a young farmer named Mendel. Mendel is a disciple of Geyer and opposes sharing the land's new riches with the Arab population. "What we have made with our own hands must remain ours," he argues. "We shall let no one take it away from us." "It would be unethical for us to deny a share in our commonwealth to any man," Littwak replies some time later, "wherever he might come from, whatever his race or creed. For we stand on the shoulders of other civilized peoples."

A ringing declaration. But what I would like Israelis to think about, and argue about in their fierce, caustic way, is what Herzl has one of the New Society's principal figures, the architect Steineck, say in response to Geyer's followers. Here *Old-New Land* has stunning relevance to the Arab-Jewish peace process. Steineck's speech about Geyer deserves to be quoted at length:

"He was an anti-Zionist rabbi! I knew him myself. He opposed us violently then also. But he gave other reasons. Oh, quite other reasons. But in one way he remained the same. Hm. I shall tell you what he was, what he is, what he will remain. He is a rabbi of the immediate advantage. When we early Zionists began to seek out our land and our people, this Dr. Geyer abused us. Yes, he called us fools and swindlers.[. . .]

"These rabbis who sought the immediate advantage made our lives a burden to us. Geyer is doing the same thing now. In those early, difficult days, he did not so much as want to hear the name of Palestine mentioned. Now he is more Palestinian than any of us. Now he is the patriot, the nationalist Jew. And we — we are the friends of the alien. If we listened to him, he would make us out to be bad Jews or even strangers in his Palestine. Yes, that's it. He wants to turn the public against us, to sow suspicion between you and us. This pious man rolls his eyes to heaven and all the time seeks his immediate advantage. In the old Ghetto days, when the rich men had all the influence, he talked to suit their notions. The nationalist-Palestinian idea made the rich men uncomfortable, and so he interpreted Judaism to suit them. He used to say then that the Jews ought not to return to their homeland, because it would upset the captains of industry and the great bankers. He and his ilk invented the myth of the Jewish mission. The function of the Jewish people was asserted to be to instruct the other peoples. Therefore, they alleged, we must live in the dispersion. Had not the other nations already hated and despised us, they would have ridiculed us for such arrogance. And Zion was not Zion! The fact was, of course, that we not only did not teach the other nations, but that they taught us — day by day and year by year — bloody, painful lessons. Finally, we roused ourselves and sought the way out of Egypt. And we found it. Then, to be sure, Dr. Geyer also came here, and brought with him all his old arrogance and hypocrisy.

"Nowadays, thank God, the Jews conduct their public affairs differently. It is not the rich alone who make the decisions, but the whole community. Communal leadership is no longer a reward for success in business. Leaders are chosen not for their wealth, but for their talent and their ability to command respect in the eyes of the public. Therefore, the instincts of the masses must be flattered. A theory for the immediate advantage of the masses must be found, or at least for what the masses imagine to be to their immediate advantage. Therefore, an anti-alien slogan is proclaimed. A non-Jew must not be accepted by the New Society. The fewer get a place near the platter, the larger the portion of each. Perhaps you believe that that is to your immediate advantage. But it is not. If you adopt that stupid, narrow-minded policy, the land will go to wrack and ruin."

As I read these lines again I become fully aware of Herzl's prophetic intelligence, his love of purity, his complete embrace of the biblical injunction from Isaiah for "perfect peace," while combining it with Nietzsche's wise recommendation, "May the future and things most distant always rule your present. What I recommend to you is not love of what is next, but love of what is distant."

It was therefore wholly appropriate that while on his voyage around Israel, Herzl visit Arab neighborhoods in Jaffa or Haifa, and travel to the Druze and Arab villages in the Galilee — places from which have come so many who have contributed so much to our country. This visit will remain a healthy corrective to those who see Herzl as Zionism's founding father, but who have neither read him, nor, what is worse, heeded his advice.

*

*   *

Meeting Arabs, Druze, Bedouins, and Circassians made Herzl feel less homesick than when in the company of his fellow Jews, who make up the majority of Israel. Yet some of these Jews have remained Jewish despite pressure from some within the heart of the Zionist movement itself. They view Judaism as standing for exile, and want nothing to do with the Jews still living the Diaspora. Those who believe in this "Canaanean myth" comprise only a tiny minority, but their ideas received wide attention during the 1930s and 1940s, and they founded a movement. The pioneers in Palestine, they believed, needed to stop calling themselves "Jews" so that they could transform themselves into "Hebrews" — inhabitants not of "Eretz Israel," but of "Eretz Ever" (the land of the Hebrew people). Itamar Ben Avi, son of Ben-Yehuda, the man most responsible for restoring spoken Hebrew, was one of the most fanatic members of the movement. Calling himself "Jebusean" (after the first inhabitants of Jerusalem), he championed the creation of a Canaanean Nation. A great admirer of Mustafa Kemal Atatürk, Ben Avi wanted to Latinize the Hebraic alphabet. Mikha Berditchevski, whom his contemporaries called the "Nietzschean Jew," defined this alternative to Zionism, "To be or not to be? To be the last Jews or the first Hebrews?"

The Canaanean Movement formulated its own answer to that thorny question, "What is a Jew?" for its members believed that Jewishness would be consigned to the shelves of history. They announced the birth of a new nation, a Hebraic nation, in which the intellectual, religious, and cultural heritage that developed during centuries of dispersion was wiped clean. Only the Jews themselves could have been capable of creating such paradoxical theories of nationality! I find it hard to imagine Czechs or Poles at the beginning of this century dreaming of freedom from the Austrians, Russians, or Germans, and suddenly declaring themselves members of a nationalistic cult whose aim is to erase their own culture and history.

Herzl always emphasized that Zionism symbolized first and foremost a return to Judaism. His point was relevant then and it is relevant today, for it reminds us that "Diaspora" and "Israel" have not always been clear about the exact nature of the bonds uniting them.

*

*   *

Herzl was not a shy man. He had plenty to discuss with the Jews he met during the rest of our trip. But I am convinced that they not only surprised him but also disconcerted him. The Jewish world has changed radically since the end of the nineteenth century, and Herzl was familiar with only a tiny part of that change. Aside from his visit to Russia, which put him into direct contact with Eastern Jews, the only Jews Herzl knew were assimilated into Western Europe. Some, including those of German origin, had contributed to the rise of the American Jewish community; there was therefore no way he could have any idea how important that community would be to Israel.

Herzl knew almost nothing about Jews from North Africa or the Middle East — though Jacques Behar, one of the delegates to the Congress of Basel, was from Algeria. To Herzl, Judaism was essentially European. It was to deal with the Jewish question in Europe that he had founded the Zionist movement.

On the other hand, Herzl was not wholly ignorant of the Sephardim. He himself was part Sephardic: on both his mother's and father's side were several ancestors who had been chased out of Spain in 1492 and who, after a long period of wandering, had settled in territories under Austrian rule. His grandfather was from Zemun, a small town near Belgrade where lived a sizable community of Jews of Spanish origin, including his mother. The town's Jewish leader was a rabbi named Yehuda Alkalay. This man of God, aware of the changes taking place, called for the creation of a Convention of the Old Ones, a kind of *more Judaico* assembly, to which fell the responsibility of preparing the "beginning of redemption." A proponent of gradual emigration to Palestine, Yehuda Alkalay was in favor of the systematic purchase of land parcels, somewhat like a consortium founded along the lines of insurance and railway companies. Herzl would pick up on Rabbi Alkalay's idea fifty-two years later.

Herzl also gained some familiarity with the Sephardic communities through his acquaintance with several of the great families of imperial Vienna, as well as through contacts he made with the Judeo-Spanish colony that had existed in the Holy Land for centuries (and which saw itself as a kind of local aristocracy). Joseph Navon Bey, president of the Ottoman Railway Company, which owned the railroad connecting Jaffa and Jerusalem, was a member of this community. Herzl had a long discussion with him before undertaking his voyage to Palestine.

Herzl was surprised to learn that half of Israel's Jewish population are descendants of these *edot hamizrah*, those Eastern communities that for so long were misunderstood by their Western counterparts. He became well aware that he needs to revise several chapters of *Old-New Land*. In the novel, during that Passover seder celebrated in the Littwak household at Tiberias, our heroes learn from one of their hosts about the conditions forcing European Jews to emigrate to the land of their ancestors. This new flight from Egypt, similar to the one recounted in the Haggadah, is narrated by the general director of the Department of Industry of the New Society, the debonair Joseph Levy. Levy, though not physically present at the seder, is there in the form of cylinders containing recordings of his story, decrypted by means of a phonograph that sits proudly in the middle of the living room. (We may pass over the fact that use of such an instrument during Passover would have incurred the wrath of the rabbis. Herzl, apparently, could not have cared less.) For Levy and for Herzl, the exodus being organized involved only European Jews in Vienna, Paris, London, Warsaw, and Berlin.

I felt sure that as soon as he came to terms with Israel's demographics, Herzl would feel both obliged and honored to emend his novel and add accounts of the exodus of Jews from Yemen, Bukhara, Kurdistan, Damascus, Morocco, Tunisia, Algeria, Iraq, Iran, and other countries. Their epic story is part of the great Zionist adventure; they have as much claim as anyone to the historical *aliyot,* or emigration. Contact with the Sephardim also made Herzl reproach me for the fact that they have sometimes been treated as second-class citizens by their Ashkenazi compatriots, who for so long comprised a majority of the Zionist movement and were the country's ruling elite. He was furious that these Sephardim have been forced to live in squalid villages far from Israel's urban centers, and that the richness of their culture has been deliberately underappreciated in order to give greater prominence to the *Yiddishkeit* Judaism so cherished by Eastern European Jews.

I did what I could to explain matters to Herzl; I know that many of my explanations did not satisfy him. Be that as it may, we add one injustice to another by ignoring the critical role Sephardic Jews have played in the Zionist story, a story in which they were principal actors, not passive bystanders. Yet so many Israelis are guilty of doing just that when it comes to assimilating Jews from the Arab countries, where these Jews have lived for thousands of years — well before the arrival of Islam. Such an attitude is an indirect and unfortunate consequence of the Israeli-Arab conflict. Far from leaving of their free will, these Jews have been forced out of their homes, and for a long time their fate was balanced against that of Palestinian refugees forced out of their homes in 1948. The "reasoning" runs like this: "There was such-and-such a number of Palestinian refugees, but we have taken in a such-and-such number of Jewish refugees from Arab countries. Let's call it even."

This kind of balance-sheet thinking is distasteful. I do not deny — far from it — that Israel's creation provoked violent outbursts of Judeophobia in Muslim countries, outbursts that continue to this day, and that this has made it difficult, even impossible, for these countries to permit significant Jewish minorities from remaining in their midst. But to say that this explains why Jews have emigrated to Israel from Arab counties is to betray history — a crime for which Jews have too often had to pay dearly. It misses the essential element behind this massive migration — the spiritual or ideological element. Jews were not forced out of Morocco, Yemen, or Tunisia; they *chose* to go to Israel, once a state had been formed. To them it was the fulfillment of their dream of a Zionism that was less political — as was the case in Europe at the end of the nineteenth century — than spiritual. Sephardic Zionism was based on the belief that their diasporic existence was temporary, however long it lasted; and that their long exile would end as soon as Israel, established according to Talmudic tradition, became completely independent.

In other words, the Sephardim were adhering to the very essence of Judaism, and were therefore no different from pious Jews from Russian and Poland who, in opposition to the rabbinical hierarchy at the time, viewed the

Zionist ideal as the fulfillment of the ancient prophecies. Whether Sephardi or Ashkenazi, these Jews, unwilling to bend their faith, adopted the spirit of a letter addressed to Herzl at the opening of the Congress of Basel by Rabbi Samuel Mohliver:

> For two thousand years we have been praying for a Redeemer who will deliver us from bitter exile and gather up all our people dispersed to the four corners of the earth. This faith lives powerfully within us; in times of misery it has been our consolation.
>
> Instead of pursuing a confused progression into strange countries, we must become one people in the truest sense of that word. Instead of being the laughing-stock of nations, we must regain respect and dignity. Such is the faith, such is the hope, behind every word uttered by our prophets and our doctors; and our people believe. Let it not be said our heart is closed to other nations, and that we believe any less than they in the universal promises made by our prophets.
>
> In truth, what our people honor and praise is not dependent solely on nationalities, nor does it reside in the joys and delights of our communities. Therefore only injustice will be mute, ill will will disappear like smoke, and the rule of evil will depart from the Earth.
>
> May God, rock and savior of Israel, fulfill his word, *"Yes I will gather my people from the East and land of the Setting Sun; and I shall bring them to Jerusalem; they will be My people, and I will be their God in truth and justice."*

I love this letter, not only because of the expression "rock of Israel" — which David Ben-Gurion would use again in the Declaration of Independence — but because it could have been written in any period, whether in Europe, Asia, or North Africa, and by any Jew faithful to the ways of our fathers. Ashkenazim and Sephardim share a community of destiny and thought. And because of the rise in intercommunity marriages in Israel, a new population of Jews is emerging, a population of which Herzl, given his mixed origins, was a member without realizing it — "Sepharnasim."

We need to be careful about something. Jewish emigration to Israel has involved more than "Ashkenazi" and "Sephardi," which are terms that refer to religious categories more than to ethnic differences. Certain Polish Jews, for example, pray according to the Sephardic rituals introduced into their communities in the sixteenth century.

The "gathering of the exiles" in Israel has involved Jewish communities throughout the world, including those long forgotten because of time and distance. Take the example of Jews who emigrated from the emirate of Bukhara, located in the heart of central Asia. Bukhara's Jews had at one point believed they were the last vestiges of the ancient land. (Imagine their surprise when they discovered that there were Jews serving in the czar's army. Called "cantonists," these Jews had been pressed into military service, and condemned to spend twenty-five years away from their families.) A good number of Bukhara's Jews made their way to Jerusalem, where they founded a synagogue that remains active to this day. Their Zionist faith was no less deep than that of Jews from China, or for that matter of Jews from the Indian subcontinent — the "Bnei Israelis" — who somehow managed to keep their faith intact over the course of the centuries. To the land of Israel came the descendants of the mountaineering Jewish tribes of the Caucasus, and Jews from Lithuania and the Crimea, separated from their synagogue since the ninth century but whose prayers still turned toward Jerusalem.

This patchwork of origins is one of Israel's great treasures — if not its greatest treasure. It is what I love about my people, a love that surges up in my breast when I least expect it. Herzl found he had no trouble appreciating Israel's riches. He was pleasantly amazed, observing conversations in cafés and restaurants and hotel lobbies: Lebanese Jews talking in French about their life in Beirut; Poles speaking in Yiddish about their childhoods in the shtetls of Volhynia or Galicia; Moroccans and Tunisians still sighing over the languorous evenings spent at parties in Casablanca or Carthage; Zimbabweans laughing as they recalled the parties organized by the Zionist club of Bulawayo; Iraqis remembering the succulent fish they ate on the banks of the Euphrates; old Germans debating the literary merits of Heine or Hölderlin; Americans boasting about their vacations in the Catskills; Russians reciting Pushkin and praising Chekhov. All this talk took place under the eyes of their children, born or settled in Israel. Behind these fragments of conversation lie stories that more often than not are epic, singular, and extraordinary. This is without doubt what gives this people, my people, the unquenchable appetite for life that gives Israel its humanity.

This "gathering of the exiles" is far from complete. So long as one Jew continues to live the Diaspora, the Zionist dream will not have been realized. That dream must embrace all Jews, including those whose existence had nearly been forgotten. Such was the case in the 1980s with the large exodus of black Jews from Ethiopia (possibly the descendants of the Queen of Sheba and King Solomon) whose earlier wanderings had left them on the Gondar and Tigrean plateaus of Ethiopia. Their villages consisted of small huts with straw roofs, within which the faithful gathered to pray or to read the scrolls written in an ancient tongue. By celebrating the Sabbath, fasting during Yom Kippur, and following the dietary laws, Ethiopian Jews stubbornly held to the faith of their ancestors, despite all the humiliations and the persecutions.

In the sixteenth century one particularly audacious Ethiopian Jew wrote one of the most singular pages in all of Jewish history, even perhaps in all of diplomatic history. David Reubeni, as he called himself, managed to make his way to Europe, where he declared himself a member of Reuben's tribe — one of the ten tribes lost following the destruction of the First Temple. He told the Europeans that he had been sent by the leaders of his tribe to negotiate a military and political alliance with the Western monarchies against the "Great Turk," in order to win back the holy lands. His arrival happened to coincide with a messianic fervor provoked by the expulsion of Jews from Spain. Reubeni was given a tumultuous welcome by the Italian Jewish communities and by the Marrano peoples on the Iberian peninsula, who were persuaded that their hour of deliverance had arrived. Joined by Diego Pires, alias Solomon Malka, the son of the king of Portugal's doctor, Reubeni managed to interest Charles V and the papacy before being burned at the stake, a victim of the Inquisition. In his way, Reubeni was Herzl's forerunner, an adventurer and visionary who sensed that the rebirth of Ancient Israel was inevitable.

Following Reubeni's death, little more was heard from the Ethiopian Jews until their "rediscovery" at the end of the nineteenth century by a delegation of scholars sent out by the Universal Israelite Alliance of Paris. Yet it wasn't until Ethiopia, like much of Africa, was gripped in the great famine in the mid-1960s that the Jewish world began taking notice of the plight of their far-flung brethren. A gigantic secret operation was mounted to bring these Jews to Israel. The operation brought out fifteen thousand before it was halted because of intelligence leaks. It resumed in June of 1991, when the Marxist government led by Mengistu, the "Red Negus," was about to topple. To prepare for his own glorious exile, Mengistu had authorized the departure of thousands of Jewish refugees from Addis Ababa in exchange for considerable amounts of money. Within days, squadrons of planes left

Israel for the Ethiopian capital to bring these Jews to their ancestral home. Israel was simply doing its duty, but what other country in the world would have felt so deep an obligation to assist such distant relatives? What other country in the world would have called upon its generous benefactors, themselves dispersed throughout the world, to help finance the settlement and integration of thousands of destitute people?

I didn't need to explain this to Herzl. He understood instinctively that such efforts are part of the Zionist dream, and that despite the difference in languages, opinions, rituals, customs, and skin color, the idea that unites all Jews is the belief that Zion is the "foundation, a stone, a tested stone, a precious cornerstone, of a sure foundation" (Isaiah, 28:16).

All this does not mean Israelis lack an identity, even though theirs is the only country in the world half of whose population — now over fifty years after its creation — was born outside Israel, and whose maternal tongue is not the country's official language. Israeli Jews are a veritable mosaic of all the races. They are blond haired and blue eyed, or black with braided hair, or brunettes with brown eyes, or Indians with copper skin.

"Israel has one and only one problem," I said to Herzl, as I often do to foreigners with whom I talk.

"And that is?"

"We can't decide what color our skin should be. We have not succeeded in deciding upon a single skin color and we doubtless never will — as anyone can see by looking at the Sabras."

Interestingly, Herzl had himself foreseen the singular mutations that would take place in the space of one or two generations. In *Old-New Land*, he speculated joyously about what the inhabitants of the New Society would be like in 1923. Where once young Jews were hairless, scrawny, and frightened, now, like plants allowed to put down roots in native soil and given sunlight, they flower. This has happened. A new type of Jew has been born, one different from those earlier Jews as described by both Judaism's friends and enemies. Still, as Ecclesiastes tells us, "there is nothing new under the sun." Indeed, by looking carefully at our institutions and listening to our squabbles, Herzl realized instantly that the weight of the past hangs heavily upon us.

5

PASSIONS

"Why is everybody wearing a military uniform?" During our walks through the streets of Jerusalem, Tel Aviv, and Haifa, my companion barraged me with questions about the enormous number of young people — girls as well as boys — and adults we saw in military garb, some of them with machine guns slung over their shoulders.

"They are recruits or reservists in the 'Tsahal' or IDF, Israel's defense force." I replied. "And if you are surprised to learn that women serve in the military, you might remember the warrior Deborah, a prophetess in the Bible, or the Jewish queen of the Berbers from the Algerian Aurès who fought against the Arab conquerors at the head of her tribe."

I'm afraid this did not convince him, however. Herzl was no feminist. The place for a mother or wife was in the home, and as a good Jewish son he knew very well the considerable power the *yiddishe mammes* wielded over the household. He had to defend his point of view in modern Israel. Men and women in Israel are now on absolutely equal footing: everyone does military service and anyone can achieve any elective office, including prime minister, as Golda Meir proved.

The presence of female soldiers shocked Herzl less than the fact that we have an army at all. It isn't that Herzl was vehemently antimilitary. Indeed, as a loyal subject of Franz Joseph, he admired military prowess. While a student at the University of Vienna, Herzl joined one the many fraternities whose adherents loved drinking and then fighting duels over offenses they had probably imagined. Unlike Alfred Dreyfus, however, Herzl chose not to join the military to prove how assimilated he was into mainstream culture. But he also did not condemn Jews in France, Austria, or elsewhere who maintained the tradition of the warlike Maccabees by covering themselves with glory on the fields of battle. Russian, Romanian, and Polish Jews often felt an instinctive aversion to military service; they considered it a *goyishe nachess* (a diversion for non-Jews), to which it was best not to sacrifice one's life. Herzl agreed.

Yet one of his first and most enthusiastic supporters was a Colonel Albert Edward Williamson Goldsmidt, a loyal servant of Queen Victoria, a highly respected lawyer, and a former officer in the Indian army. Therefore it wasn't from unthinking antimilitarism that Herzl regretted

Israel's having an army. He was disappointed because he had imagined that in his New Society there would, strictly speaking, be no need for one. He kept in mind a line from *Pirké Avot* (the title of a collection of rabbinical proverbs called *The Sayings of the Fathers*, incorporated in the Talmud), "The world values three things — law, truth, and peace." Like others of his time, Herzl was persuaded that the age of reconciliation and peaceful coexistence among all the peoples in the world had arrived. In the Jewish state of his dreams, events would proceed according to Isaiah's lyrical prophecies — swords would be hammered into plowshares and the lambs would lie down with wolves. He was convinced that maintaining an army in the New Society was senseless. Every citizen would, however, be required to spend two years doing public service following completion of his studies. Herzl envisioned this kind of civil conscription as a way of combining social and athletic activities. He subscribed to the theories of Friedrich Jahn and others on the virtues of gymnastics; he believed in sporting events. This is why he makes one of his protagonists say in *Old-New Land:*

> Our State will look nothing at all like the European States that you have known. We are a bourgeois society, but one that seeks nothing more than what work and culture can provide us. We want our youth to be vigorously physical, because we cultivate our bodies as well as our minds.

Mens sana in corpore sano, a healthy body means a healthy mind. The author of *The Jewish State* had conscientiously kept in mind the lessons taught him by the classical authors. To those lessons he added his own thoughts about the physical and moral "degeneration" of Jews living in the ghettos — a notion that was widespread at the time, expressed among others by his friends the Viennese doctor Max Nordau and the Jewish Italian sociologist Cesare Lumbroso, both of whom were among the earliest adherents to the Zionist movement.

History does not always automatically follow the rules laid down by intellectuals and prophets. History has always reserved the right to decide otherwise. Because Israel's neighbors refuse to accord us the simple right to exist, we have had to wage wars, five in all, to assure our country's survival. To bring this point home to Herzl I took him to the sites that symbolize what we have had to face since 1948. The first we saw from the train taking us from Tel Aviv to Jerusalem. Atop a hill was a strange-looking construction, partly gigantic antenna and partly futuristic sculpture. It is a monument erected to the memory of Israeli Air Force pilots killed during the war. The second site we saw as we made our way toward Jerusalem from David's City. Near Shaar Hagay, where the steep climb to Jerusalem begins, one can see ocher-colored automobile wreckage strewn along the road. These are the remnants of the armored cars destroyed in 1947 and 1948, when our enemies were laying siege to the Holy City. To feed the trapped Jewish inhabitants, convoys left daily from Tel Aviv; few survived intact. I explained to Herzl the whole fearful period of the "Birmany Road," constructed in a matter of days by volunteers so that the soldiers and civilians in Jerusalem might get the relief they needed so desperately.

Then I filled Herzl in about David Ben-Gurion, and his gargantuan efforts to ensure that Israel would not be crushed by those assailing it. Even before the Declaration of Independence, Ben-Gurion had known that if Israel did not have arms and an army it would not come into existence. Working tirelessly with his colleagues, he assembled the Tsahal, mustered in a matter of only weeks using recruits with no experience whatever in military matters. Tsahal's numbers were dwarfed by the forces levied by the enemies of Zionism. At the time, the ratio between the Jewish population of Yichov and the Arab population was one to seven. Moreover, our ragged band of soldiers lacked the most essential thing of all: guns. The United States had recognized Israel's statehood, but not provided the rifles we needed to defend it. Furnishing the soldiers with uniforms and rifles and ammunition put our leaders to an extreme test. Israel did not even have a budget. And arms dealers are not known for offering credit. They want cash, huge piles of it.

Gifts flowed in from every corner of the Diaspora. Golda Meir went to the United States with ten dollars in her pocket and returned with millions — the famous "Stephens" as they were called, in honor of their provider, the American Zionist leader Rabbi Stephen Wise. But we would have fought to defend our newborn country, dollars or no dollars.

A miracle was needed; a miracle happened. And the name of that miracle is the Tsahal — the army that would never retreat, whatever the cost. The War of Independence cost the lives of six thousand Israeli soldiers, or roughly one percent of the population. During the other wars we waged — the Suez War, the Six-Day War, the Yom Kippur War, and the War in Lebanon — we have had to pay dearly in human lives. Nearly every Israeli family has lost someone.

Our survival owes more than I can say to the Tsahal's extraordinary effectiveness. Ben-Gurion used to say with a smile, "I do not know if the Tsahal is the best army in the world, but I don't know of a better one." He was right many thousand times over. Israel has produced soldiers and officers of great valor. Its air force is among the most sophisticated and best trained in the world, as are its infantry, tank divisions, parachute divisions, and navy. The Israeli military is among the most modern in part because of assistance from the United States, in part because we have developed our own arms industry, permitting us to manufacture tanks, cannons, and missiles. Scientific research of the highest level has given us two nuclear reactors.

"Kol hakavod le Tsahal!" ("Hooray for Tsahal!"), Herzl exclaimed when I finished.

But with his typically Viennese *witz*, or sense of humor, he added, "Though I do also wonder if you aren't becoming a sort of Junker Jew, with all your boasting about Israel's military."

"The army has played a decisive role in our nation's history," I replied, "but that role is circumscribed. The Tsahal is an army of citizen-soldiers, an army in which nearly every Israeli over eighteen, regardless of gender, serves for three years — twenty months in the case of women — and for yearly periods of varying length in the reserves. That much is true. But the army does not constitute a state within the state; it has not given rise to a military caste. It has not given rise to a Middle Eastern version of the Junkers. Just the opposite. In Israel, the generals in the reserves are principal actors in the peace process. They can speak with authority because they have seen firsthand how cruel and inhuman war can be."

Herzl seemed skeptical, so I gave him an example — the finest example I could think of.

"A former member of the Palmach — an elite unit of the Haganah, the precursor to the Tsahal — and commander in chief of the army during the Six-Day War, Yitzhak Rabin was the signatory prime minister, along with me, of the historic peace accords made with Yasser Arafat's PLO and King Hussein of Jordan. Rabin knew that the final offensive, the riskiest and most audacious campaign of them all, would be the fight for peace. He ended his speech at the enormous pro-peace rally at Kings Square in Tel Aviv on November 4, 1995, by giving his army serial number. Minutes later he was shot to death. The Israeli general who had saved the country from annihilation was killed while leading the forces of democracy."

I tried to convince Herzl that Israel truly is exceptional — and that its democratic system is all the more remarkable when we remember that military regimes are commonplace in the Middle East. Though we have had to fight constantly to ensure our existence, we have obstinately refused to accept a military government. A military coup d'etat was not a danger against which Israel was by some miracle forearmed — especially since at the very heart of our society are groups who would welcome a military regime, who believe generals should wield power over civilians. The tumultuous history of the Holy Land has created redoubtable precedents for their way of thinking.

"You will understand my point better when we see the fortifications at Caesarea and the magnificent Crusader castle on the coast at Acre," I told Herzl.

There we saw the remains of those fearless young Crusaders who defended their hold on parts of the Levant, trying to survive in a hostile environment far from their homes — and from the religious zealousness that sent them there to begin with. Wandering the length of Acre's battlements, I remarked that it was no coincidence the world's experts on Crusader sites are the Israeli medievalists Arié Graboïs and Joshua Prawer, whose work has proven relevant to contemporary events. Analyzing the Crusader fortifications helped us avoid the tragic fate that befell them.

"We have a democracy behind us," I concluded. "And that is our most effective fortification by far."

Israel has followed some of the recommendations

Herzl made in *The Jewish State* — stationing the army in barracks, for example — but I had to seek his forgiveness that we did not follow his suggestion about the national flag. Herzl had wanted a white flag, with seven gold stars, in which "the color white represents a new life, a pure life, and the stars stand for the seven hours of our working day. For it is beneath the symbol of work that Jews will make the new country."

Those who succeeded Herzl at the helm of the Zionist movement preferred a blue and white flag with the Star of David set in the middle, the star having for generations been the symbol of Judaism. What became our national flag existed before 1948. It flew over the roofs of the Warsaw ghetto during the uprising in April 1943. At the risk of making Herzl (and others) laugh, I told him that before 1948 that same flag was referred to as the "Palestinian flag," and that General Koenig, a hero of Free France, flew its colors on his car, next to his personal banner, in homage to the Palestinian Jews who had fought by his side at the battle of Bir Hacheim in North Africa. During the British occupation, the "Palestinian flag" waved proudly over certain buildings in a show of defiance and pride. A former prime minister of Israel risked arrest by raising its colors. In the Middle East words have double-edged meanings. Whatever the history and nomenclature, the blue and white banner has become our country's official symbol, and my heart swells with pride when I gaze upon it.

*

*   *

Our political system provided plenty of surprises for Herzl. He himself had strong political feelings, and they stood in stark contrast to the liberal, radical, or social democratic positions held by many Austrian, German, and French Jews. An admirer of the Austro-Hungarian monarchy and suspicious of revolutionary ardor, Herzl believed that "the democratic aristocracy and the aristocratic republic represented the best forms of government." He was convinced that governance was far too serious a matter to be left up to the general population; governing should go from the top down, not the other way around. His vision for the Jewish state was therefore as a sort of aristocratic republic, based upon a constitution that was oligarchic in nature — somewhat after the model of the Venetian doges.

Herzl was skeptical when I explained some of the complexities of Israeli politics, and the judicial acrobatics that went into establishing its government. Israel is one of the only countries in the world — perhaps the only one — whose government remains shrouded in mystery. The Declaration of Independence, read out loud by an emotional David Ben-Gurion on May 14, 1948, in a museum room in Tel Aviv, affirms that a Jewish state was being created in Eretz Israel by virtue of the "traditional historical ties" between the Jews and the Promised Land. The Declaration evokes the people's "natural rights" to a nation that, "like all nations," had earned the right to be "master of its destiny on earth and over its sovereignty."

Assured of protection in the "rock of Israel" — a

phrase intended to satisfy both religious and secular sensibilities — the Declaration also affirms that this new country is founded upon the principles of the Charter of the United Nations, and that it will recognize "complete social and political equality for all citizens, regardless of religion, race, or sex, and guarantees the freedoms of assembly, conscience, language, education, and culture; it also assures the protection of holy places of all the religions." What the Declaration doesn't makes clear is whether the country is a republic or a monarchy.

This ambiguity would not be clarified by the time the first Knesset met on February 16, 1949, or when the Transition Law was enacted, establishing the state's ruling structure. All that was clear was that at the head of the government would be a president — a president of the government and not a president of the republic, as in America — and that the country would be led by a prime minister appointed by the Knesset, whose members were to be elected by popular vote for a four-year term.

"I am afraid I did not dwell much on a system of government in my books," Herzl told me.

I confessed that reading his books indeed made it difficult to figure out what sort of government he foresaw for his New Society.

"But I have to tell you that I find the absence of a constitution deeply disturbing."

I agreed with him. Then I tried to explain the reasons.

"The deliberations of the first Knesset ended with

this stunning realization: given the impossibility of arriving at a consensus between the religious factions, for whom the fundamental law of the state must be the Torah, and the secular factions, which constitute a majority in the country, it was wiser not to have any constitution at all. In its place — though not fulfilling its functions — was the 1949 Transition Law, which contains the few constitutional matters on which there was consensus. No doubt I risk indignation by pointing out that Great Britain, a model of parliamentary democracy, does not have a constitution either."

"True," replied Herzl, "though it was also not endowed with a constituent assembly."

I tried a different tack.

"Well, perhaps it just shows our Shalom Aleichem side."

"Please explain."

In his vivid depictions of life in the Russo-Polish shtetlach, I told Herzl, this grandfather of Yiddish literature showed how all the Jewish settlements around 1905 were noisily arguing about the magic word "constitution." It all involved a manifesto Czar Nicholas II was going to accord his loyal subjects. Jews waited for this new constitution with bated breath. They thought it would put an end to their sufferings in Russia. What they got instead was revolution, and then after revolution the reestablishment of an autocracy. As one of the inhabitants of Kasrilevke — a shtetl with Shalom Aleichemesque predilections — says, "Why do you think the Jews will do what even the czar couldn't?" Some disappointed souls grumble that the Israeli constitution is like the Messiah: we will be condemned to wait for it until the end of time.

*

*   *

Political squabbling has not prevented our country from facing up to its responsibilities, or kept our citizens from building a homeland that takes in hundreds of thousands of immigrants from countries with political systems vastly different from ours. Herzl pardoned Israel its childhood afflictions. On the other hand, I was a little concerned about his reactions when we took advantage of our stay in Jerusalem and attended a session of the Knesset.

The Knesset faces the Israel Museum, which houses the Dead Sea scrolls. Visiting it was a kind of obligation for my companion. As Paris correspondent for the Viennese *Neue Freie Presse,* Herzl conscientiously attended meetings of the Chambres des Députés, or national assembly, and regularly supplied colorful descriptions of the French parliamentary debates at a time when Clemenceau and Jaurès were in full-throated oratory. Some of his articles were recently republished in France under the title *The Bourbon Palace: Scenes of French Parliamentary Life* and provide an invaluable eyewitness account of political life during the Third Republic. Herzl was an excellent reporter. He knew how to get to the source, he won the confidence of many of the key figures, and he had no equal in his ability to analyze a political crisis — particularly when it was over some trivial matter. French politicians feared Herzl's pen and his ferocity. Many were relieved when he left Paris to pursue his lunatic dream of founding a Jewish state.

Arriving at the Knesset, equipped with an official pass and all the necessary credentials, Herzl felt reconnected to his journalistic youth.

"I am hoping," he confessed, "that I will be reminded of the scenes I used to witness in the Palais Bourbon." His eyes were shining.

"Well, to begin with, what do you think of the architecture?"

The Knesset is a large gray concrete edifice whose columns come rising up from the Judean Hills. The semicircular main hall may seem singularly empty to him. A single speaker might be addressing a handful of delegates manifestly preoccupied with something else. Perhaps only one of his colleagues and the president will be listening to him.

"The setting is beautiful. And I admire that tapestry."

He was pointing to a giant Chagall tapestry.

Though he said nothing, I also caught Herzl staring at the enormous portrait of him done by the artist Dani Caravan, hanging in the hall. I used to go to the Knesset to watch the portrait being done. It is only appropriate Herzl's portrait should hang there. The Knesset, after all, is the successor to the Congress of Basel.

What surprised Herzl first was the presence of religious delegates. The idea that rabbis might involve themselves in the country's political workings seemed completely strange to him. In *The Jewish State*, he articulates clearly his rejection of a theocratic system:

> Faith unites us, knowledge gives us freedom. We shall therefore prevent any theocratic tendencies from coming to the fore on the part of our priesthood. We shall keep our priests within the confines of their temples in the same way as we shall keep our professional army within the confines of their barracks. Army and priesthood shall receive honors high as their valuable functions deserve. But they must not interfere in the administration of the State which confers distinction upon them, else they will conjure up difficulties without and within.

Again Herzl proved visionary. He sternly disapproved of the role religious parties play in governing Israel today, viewing them as representing the resurgence of the movement founded by the infamous Doctor Geyer, a movement to which, as we've seen, he was vehemently opposed. When he has the architect Steineck recall ironically that this Geyer had once been hostile to Zionism (which Geyer saw as a renewal of the abominations of Canaan), Herzl would never have imagined that his words would be so relevant at the turn of the millennium. There are certainly politically active religious parties whose members are engaged constructively in matters of state; there are others who remain vigorously hostile to the very ideology on which Israel was founded. Yet their hostility stops short of their calling for the government to bend to their demands and to their profoundly theocratic approach to matters.

"Yeshiva students, who were exempted from military service, did not also lose the right to vote, and thereby to influence the direction of the country to which they are unwilling to sacrifice their lives," I told Herzl.

"Perhaps," he replied, "you should unleash a new *Kulturkampf,* so as to eradicate the influence of religious factions in the country's governance."

I remembered Herzl was an admirer of Bismarck.

"We have had to make compromises," I said. "And to justify those compromises I think about my grandfather. He was a pious and just man. I used to go and pray with him at the synagogue in Vichneva. And I always used to remember him when I was negotiating with the religious factions. Whenever I had to make a decision touching upon the relationship between religion and state, I asked myself whether grandfather would agree with what I'd done."

I gave as an example when I negotiated with the religious factions over their yeshivas and the privileges and exceptions being accorded their students. The rabbis who run the schools explained that these institutions had existed throughout the Diaspora. What a paradox it would be, they argued, were Israel to be the only state in the world denying religious communities the right to form rabbinical schools, and refusing to exempt their students from military service. *Toratam oumanatam,* they said. "Studying the Torah is their profession." Recalling my youth in Vishneva, and my grandfather, I had to agree.

"Anyway," I concluded, "I do not believe I have caused my grandfather any posthumous disappointment."

I emphasized to Herzl that I was still in favor of taking religion out of politics. I have too much respect for God to transform Him into an arbitrator of our petty squabbles. I am always surprised when those who view figures in the Enlightenment (and their conception of God as the Great Clock Maker) as profoundly impious, themselves view the Eternal Being as a sort of Great Surveyor, measuring every last square inch of Israel, or as a Great Court Clerk, recording the sins and faults committed in His eyes by the Jews. My vision of the sacred is less trivial.

Because I believe in Judaism and its values so deeply, I am concerned about the growing schism between the religious and the secular factions in Israel. The former, to be quite honest, have proven themselves far more vindictive than the latter. If we are not careful, this latent conflict could divide Israel and Israeli society, and encourage intolerance and discourage progress. Any attempt to reduce Judaism to a kind of excessive ritualism represents an intellectual and spiritual poverty that is out of character with the nature and genius of our nation. We could therefore do worse than solicit some advice from the clear-headed founder of the Zionist movement.

*

*   *

That is why I made a point of taking Herzl to the Knesset. I did this with some trepidation, for however mixed my own feelings about the presence of religious factions in the semicircle, I was afraid what Herzl would subsequently write would flatter none of us. Debates in the Knesset rarely do honor to Israeli democracy. This was noted even during the country's early days. An American journalist was once surprised to see an enormous pile of pending matters stacked up on the desk of Yossef Sprinzak, the Knesset's first speaker. "Don't tell me that you're actually going to vote on all those issues!" the American exclaimed. "What do you mean?" replied Sprinzk. "We have two thousand years to make up for."

Herzl was clearly pained by some Knesset sessions, during which insults and recriminations flew around the semicircle, making the atmosphere almost circuslike.

"I'm the first to regret the absence, or extreme rarity, of parliamentary decorum," I agreed, "let alone of sessions that deserve mention in the annals of history. But let me hasten to add that there have been shining exceptions, such as when David Ben-Gurion announced the capture of Adolf Eichmann, or the historic speech President Anwar as-Sadat gave to the delegates in 1977. There was also that wonderful and precious moment of national unity when it came time to pass the law calling for the reunification of Jerusalem."

Alas, I had to admit to Herzl, for every moment of dignity there have been many more of shrillness and silliness. Sometimes arguments have even degenerated into physical confrontations — right on the floor of the Knesset. It is one of the plagues of contemporary life in Israel, connected perhaps to our habit of blowing things out of proportion and living on the extremes. This is what the writer Amos Oz calls the "Chekhov side" to our character. Israelis, he believes, prefer Chekhov to Shakespeare when it comes to tragedy. Shakespeare's characters choose a course of action and then tear themselves apart pursuing it, always dying in the play's last act; Chekhov's characters tear each other apart — but no course of action gets chosen and nobody dies. Instead, everyone ends up exhausted, more indolent and desperate than when the curtain went up, unable to make even the smallest decision, contenting themselves with mediocre solutions and pathetic compromises.

This situation is a direct consequence of our political and electoral system, which is marked by the sharp polarization of right and left, and by the complete impossibility of any politician achieving a clear majority in the Knesset. Every government since 1948 has had to rely upon coalitions of varying solidity. Within some of these coalitions the good of the country appears less important than the good of the individual faction.

Quarreling and rivalry characterize both ends of the political spectrum, deepening even further the normal division between right wing and left wing. So fierce an adversary of Menachem Begin was David Ben-Gurion that he never even deigned to mention Begin's name. Instead, he would refer to Begin as "the man sitting to the right of Deputy Bader." He also did endless battle with Levi Eshkol, a fellow member of the Labor Party. After Eshkol's death, several of his friends tried to get Ben-Gurion to attend the funeral; after all, Eshkol had been prime minister of Israel during the Six-Day War. Ben-Gurion's reply is legendary. "I will not. Moreover I refuse to allow him to attend my funeral." This same Ben-Gurion, the man often called the "father of the country," was himself ostracized by his colleagues, who forced him out of power, though he could have continued to govern for much longer (and for the good of our country, in my opinion).

What more is there to say about all this political strife, except that the most urgent task facing the members of any parliamentary majority, whoever the prime minister may be, must be the peace process? On the budget issue, we were witness to singular negotiations between the heads of the various parliamentary factions, each making their vote contingent upon funding for their schools or their institutions. Given what is truly at stake today in the Middle East, this kind of debate has not lifted the quality of our political life. Herzl deplored our preoccupation with unimportant matters. In 1977, Yitzhak Rabin was forced to resign as prime minister not because he found himself in a minority in a vote of confidence involving some vital issue of national security, but because his wife had neglected to close a bank account she had opened when her husband was the Israeli ambassador to the United States.

"There was a time," I told Herzl, half in wonder at the memory of it, "when the Israeli government's ability to lead depended upon the arrival times of El Al flights on Friday afternoons."

Herzl looked nonplussed.

"Were one plane to land one or two minutes into shabbat, a party or a delegate could use it as a pretext for bringing a motion of censure, destroying the power coalition, and even provoking new elections. That by itself should demonstrate how difficult it was to govern with any assurance; every head of government was at the mercy of a vote of censure."

"An unacceptable situation," Herzl added sympathetically.

"Yes, everyone clamored for a change. So we had change."

I explained that experts in electoral matters were called in, drawn from the ranks of the finest gurus and thinkers. These experts advocated a radical — and radically lamebrained, in my view — change in the political system. Unfortunately, they managed to convince others of their idea. These sorcerer's apprentices succeeded in creating a consensus, leading to the first change in our electoral system since the Knesset adopted the Transition Law in February of 1949. Without really consulting public opinion, they changed the ballot system by separating the election of prime minister from the election of Knesset delegates. The head of the government would henceforth be elected by popular vote. This completely upset the balance of powers between the legislative and executive branches — without at the same time stabilizing governmental coalitions. We've seen the disastrous results in recent events.

The experiment had never been tried elsewhere. Rather than "squaring the circle" we were now, as it were, "rounding the triangle," which was no improvement, at least so far as governmental institutions go. I didn't hide from Herzl my strong feelings that the reforms were a terrible mistake. I do not say this lightly; if anything, where matters of error or blame are concerned, I have a tendency to relativize. To the consternation of some of my friends and colleagues, I am not among those who believe history was intended to teach us about the errors of the past. No one and nothing is infallible, and my instinct is to be suspicious of anyone who claims to be. Each of us — and I am no exception — makes mistakes; sometimes these mistakes prove beneficial. But in the matter of choosing a prime minister, I believe sincerely that we have committed a new mistake in trying to correct an older one. We have set up a presidential electoral system without a truly presidential system of government. We have removed the parliament's power to appoint a prime minister from someone among its ranks, someone active in its deliberations.

It would have been far more intelligent to reform the ballot system by substituting a proportion system, in which a certain number of delegates are elected from each territory. This is far from perfect, but it corrects excesses resulting from overrepresentation of parties with specific interests, and from those who would not hesitate to take advantage of the public vote to advance those interests.

"It would seem to me," replied Herzl, "that Israel's political system tacitly favors ethnic groupings and tribalism."

How right he was about this. Tribalism and Balkanization are the two scourges of our age. The current system permits the composition of voting lists based on ethnic origins.

One can see what happens when regional protests become uncontrollable, even in certain Western countries with long histories of stability. Imagine the danger it poses to a country such as Israel, whose population is made up of immigrants. If we are not careful, this phenomenon might have dire consequences upon our national unity, the bedrock of Jewish identity and Zionism, whose whole purpose is to unite those living in lonely exile.

"I sometimes wonder," I said to Herzl, "whether our dysfunctional political system does not stem from the simple fact that we have not yet understood what it means to build a state."

"Explain what you mean."

"With its squabbles, phony debates, minitragedies, and melodramas, political life in Israel constitutes a sort of second-rate parody of Jewish life in the shtetlach, where the *parnassim*, the community leaders, would argue endlessly about everything — what direction to take, who would receive the honors of the synagogue, who would be put in charge of which institution, et cetera — a state of affairs that persists to this day in the numerous communities of the Diaspora."

Yet I hastened to add that despite these flaws Israel remains a modern country, a state in the fullest sense of the word — not a shtetl miraculously transplanted in the Middle East. The country's founding fathers showed political genius by recreating a Jewish homeland in less than a century, and by somehow giving it the means and will to survive in a hostile environment. "Perhaps," replied Herzl, "the founding fathers were asking a great deal of their fellow Jewish citizens — some people go so far as to say they were asking far too much."

Herzl's comment struck me. I told him again of my admiration for David Ben-Gurion. Ben-Gurion put his faith in the concept of *mamlakhtiyout*, a Hebraic term with no equivalent in English, but which might be translated as "the predominance of the state's interests over those of the individual," or more simply, "reasons of state." Ben-Gurion was openly dismissive of those he suspected were not wholly devoted to the ideal. I will confess that I am enormously indebted to him in the matter.

"Naturally, an exalted view of the state and the responsibilities of political leadership can be wearying," I said to Herzl. "One evening, during negotiations with Yasser Arafat, he exclaimed, 'Ah, democracy. My God! Who invented this thing? It's so tiresome!'"

"No one can be heroic twenty-four hours a day, three hundred and sixty-five days a year," replied Herzl.

"Yes," I agreed. "And since its creation, Israel has ceaselessly been confronted with the impossible, forced to excel in everything if it is to endure."

Having been for centuries the "salt of nations" — and for that paying a heavy tribute — the Jews still cannot enjoy the luxury of serenity. The burden of history sometimes hangs heavily, very heavily, upon our shoulders; that might explain if not justify some of our mistakes and our shortcomings.

After more than half a century of existence, it would be normal and human were we to go through a slump, a low period, when our beautiful machine seems to get jammed up. To that slump we can attribute the Netanyahu government, and the slowing of the peace process. Although an agreement was reached at Wye Plantation, it was not implemented by the Netanyahu government in the face of the opposition encountered from the right-wing factions of the coalition.

"But a slump can only last for so long," I ruminated. "I am firmly convinced that governing means choosing."

I told Herzl that my feeling was that we needed to make our decisions based not on immediate self-interest or half-baked political assumptions, but because they are the only way to guarantee Israel's future — even if we feel that the cost of peace seems too high. If we do not achieve this peace, we will place the lives of our great-grandchildren in jeopardy. Those not yet born will be forced to pay for our lack of courage and unity. That insight guided me during the negotiations with the

Palestinians, and rather than an example of national chauvinism I believe it represents the highest form of patriotism.

"I inherited this belief from Ben-Gurion," I told Herzl.

"You admire him greatly."

"Yes, he was a visionary genius who knew how to distinguish the trivial from the essential, and how to project himself into the future."

I gave an example to illuminate this. Ben-Gurion thought it necessary the Knesset adopt the Law of the Return in 1950, automatically conferring Israeli nationality upon all Jews — not because we were not anticipating new waves of immigration, and not solely from a desire to reply to a malicious remark once made to him by Yossef Sprinzak.

"It was because Ben-Gurion believed that such a measure, whatever the legal rights it gave to future immigrants, connected Israel to the very spirit of Zionism, a spirit whose purpose would not simply end once Israel came into existence. He rightly sensed that at the dawn of the new millennium, Zionism, born at the end of the nineteenth century, still constituted an immense aspiration."

"I think," replied Herzl, "that you are going to tell me that events proved that he was right."

6

A YEAR IN MOSCOW

I had already tried to emphasize to Herzl that Israelis are unique.

"They come from the four corners of the earth, thrown together, more or less harmoniously, into a single nation, united by a common tongue, culture, and history, and by the desire to face the future as a people."

But Israel is constantly evolving, so much so that it would be difficult to guess what the country will be like in ten or twenty years. To anyone who doubts the truth of this — or suspects I am simply engaging in a typically Mediterranean form of exaggeration — I say, "Look at the past decade." The Israel of today bears little relation to the Israel of ten years ago. Had I traveled around Israel with Herzl a decade earlier, our voyage would have had, I believe, far less significance. This is due to one momentous event, one whose consequences Israelis still have not properly measured: the influx of immigrants from the former Soviet Union. Herzl listened in amazement as I told him of the Russian exodus, and said it exceeded any of his wildest dreams. More than nearly anyone else in his day, he was sensitive to the misery and despair of Russian Jews. And when I was in power I did everything I could to help Soviet Jewry become part of the Jewish national renaissance.

And Moses said to Pharaoh, *Shalah et ami,* "Let my people go." Both Herzl and I had repeated these same words, though several decades apart in time, to the Kremlin masters.

"Not to the same masters, of course," interrupted Herzl. "I was dealing with Nicholas II and his advisers, particularly Plehve, the minister of the interior whose hands were covered in blood from the pogroms at Kishinyov and Pobiedonotsev. Plehve, you know, had already concocted his formula about the Jews: 'A third will convert, a third will emigrate, and a third will be massacred.' "

Those of my generation confronted Stalin and his successors, founders of a new empire whose crashing demise few would have dared predict even two decades ago.

In Herzl's day, and until recently in our own, Russia was the "prison of peoples," to use the phrase of the great writer Aleksandr Herzen. For Jews, Russia was less a mother than a stepmother, submitting its adopted children to insults and blows of every kind imaginable. When they were not massacring Jews — while proclaiming, "Spaci Rossiou, beï Jidov" ("Save Russia, kill the Jews") — they were reducing them to servitude, physical or intellectual.

*

*　　*

As he walked through the streets of present-day Tel Aviv, Carmel, or Tiberias, Herzl was surprised and delighted to hear so many people speaking Russian. Once, of course, Jews tended to speak in Yiddish rather than in the language of Tolstoy or Pushkin. But that wasn't important to him. History is finally proving him right, and with his head held retrospectively high Herzl was able to throw off all the opprobrium heaped upon him during the last months of his life for having called upon — on the day after the brutal massacre in Kishinyov in 1903 — his people's executioners. He was right a thousand times over to have done what he did, for his fellow Jews were at last managing to leave the "vale of tears" for the land of their ancestors.

I understand this feeling better when I myself walk in the Beit Hakerem neighborhood of Jerusalem. On Bialik Street I sometimes hear new immigrants conversing in Russian, and I can't help thinking of the masterpiece by that great modern Hebraic poet Haim Nachman Bialik, who gave his name to this quiet, shady avenue. How could anyone be unmoved by the cry of pain and revolt contained within *The City of Slaughter*, written the day after that act of barbarism against which Tolstoy, Gorky, and Jaurès raised their voices? Bialik's verses haunt us:

In the iron, in the steel, frozen, hard, and silent
Forge a heart and may it be yours, man, and come with me!
Come to the village of the massacre, for you need to see
With your eyes, to feel with your own hands,
On the gates, fences, doors, and walls.
On the paving stones, on the stone and the wood
The dark imprint of dried blood, of brain,
The imprint of your brothers, and their heads, and their
     throats.

The Kishinyov pogrom was to Herzl's generation what the anti-Semitic Stalinist purges were to our own. In both cases, only the most clear-minded among us came to the aid of the Jews. For Herzl, a king without a kingdom, there was but one solution: go to St. Petersburg and meet with Plehve and Count Witte, the finance minister, and negotiate a massive emigration of Russian Jews to a *Nach-tasyl*, "night-time asylum," meaning the land of Israel — or by default Uganda or the Sinai, if permission could be obtained from the British Foreign Office. His initiative provoked a serious crisis within the young Zionist movement, but Herzl paid it no heed. Ever the pragmatist, he followed his hunches, for good or for bad, and was reluctant to concede defeat even when events turned against him.

Herzl's trip to Russia was planned in complete secrecy, like his visit to Palestine.

"It was one of the most significant moments of my life," he said with feeling. "You see, I was a Westerner raised in German culture. I was used to the best restaurants and the finest hotels. These trips revealed the truth about Jewish life. Far from the palaces of the Rothschilds or Baron Moritz von Hirsch, I had met with the little people of the shtetlach, the *luftmenschen* — those buffeted by the winds of their time. I saw a nation of dreamers, beggars, and indigents."

Herzl quoted lengthy extracts from his *Diary* to justify his Russian trip. Anticipating my questions, he launched into a moving description of the welcome he was given on August 17, 1903, by Russian Zionists. He finished with this request.

"Shimon Peres, I hope you will see to the Russian Jews. They are the heart and soul of our people, even if their behavior is sometimes judged harshly by their Western counterparts. I myself shared the prejudices about the *Ostjuden*, as we used to call them dismissively. I know that now. At Vilna, in Russian Lithuania, the police who were watching me very closely had forbidden any rallies around my visit, but police or no, the crowds pressed in closely to show their affection."

In reply, I told Herzl that Golda Meir could have described her visit to the synagogue in Moscow in 1948 in much the same way he describes his 1903 trip. She had been named Israel's first ambassador to the USSR. This was during Stalin's time, when even the slightest contact with an outsider could condemn a Soviet citizen to years in a Soviet gulag. But tens of thousands of Jews, some from Central Asia, gathered around the building located behind Red Square to show their joy and their pride. Thousand and thousands of nameless people came out, their eyes red with tears, braving the dreaded Beria's police, just as their parents and grandparents had defied the Okhrana, the czarist police, in Vilna. It was completely unexpected — and weighty with significance for the young Jewish state. Meir's visit is commemorated on an Israeli banknote that shows a gathering of Jews, their faces retouched to protect their identity — a rather singular way of printing money, and one that could only have happened in Israel.

Other Israelis who visited Russian between 1948 and 1991, going to the dark heart of the old anti-Semite demons, saw something of what Herzl and Golda Meir experienced. They were accosted by Jews who had applied for or wanted to apply for the right to emigrate to Israel, and bombarded with questions. Russian Jews were dying to know things about Israel that official propaganda had kept from them.

"I too have seen history change course with my own eyes," I said to Herzl. "I had never expected to live to see the day when I might return to my native Belarus, which had been Polish until 1939, when it was annexed by the Soviet Union as part of the Hitler-Stalin pact. But in 1992 I did return."

"Tell me the story."

I explained that it was an official visit — I was Israel's

foreign minister — but I went to Vichneva, the small town of my childhood. No Jews live there now. All of them, including my grandparents and so many members of my family, were exterminated by the Germans, burned alive in the local synagogue, which was made of wood. A pile of stones marks the ditch into which their remains were thrown. There is no other commemoration. The houses in the village were all destroyed, replaced by Soviet-style brick and cement structures. Only the well in the town square is still there, directly in front of the place where my parents lived through this time of darkness and evil. I drank water from the well, and its taste awakened a host of memories buried deep inside me. But I had to face the truth: nothing remained of the places of my youth, nothing to welcome me back and evoke a past that I had nonetheless refused to believe was gone entirely.

In Vologda Oblast, the region where my mother, née Meltzer, was born, things were not much different. A few Jews came forward to greet me. Some were thrilled at the idea of meeting an Israeli minister, a modern equivalent of one of these envoys from the Holy Land who in the eighteenth and nineteenth centuries used to travel through towns and villages of the Diaspora, raising money for the Jewish communities in Jerusalem, Tiberias, Safed, and Hebron. Some of them had family members who had emigrated to Israel years earlier; the younger ones hoped to rejoin them. Others claimed they had known my father and my grandfather, though I couldn't say whether they were telling the truth or simply wanted to please me.

They were survivors in every sense of the word. They had survived the Nazis and they had survived Stalin's purges, watching helplessly while their world crumbled around them.

The old yeshiva in Volojin, renowned as a training ground for philosophers, had been transformed into a bakery. Furnaces, platforms, and kneading machines had replaced the shelves filled with Talmuds and works of rabbinical jurisprudence. Only a bas-relief, showing the tablets of the Law, showed what the place had once been. One could make out, written in Hebrew, "Volojin Yeshiva, founded in 1803."

In the cemetery, long since abandoned, eight tombstones still carried the names of my paternal family, the Perskis. As for the Meltzer house, it was still there. An old Ukrainian peasant welcomed me in. She mistook me for an official of the Belarus Republic — then recently created — and proceeded to complain. "My husband is sick. The price of vegetables has never been so low. Please, *natchalnik* [director], help us a little."

Her calling me "natchalnik" made me smile. Eighty years earlier, were she addressing a member of the czar's government, she would have said, "Vacha Vissokaïa Blagodarnost," "Your High Nobility," and then followed it with a similar litany of complaint. It was as if history had been frozen, as if nothing had happened between my departure for Palestine and 1992, or more exactly — since we are talking about the Soviet Union and Russia — between 1917 and today. The peasants still want "land and bread"; as for the Jews, persecuted at regular intervals, they have survived it all, hoping that one day they might see the Jerusalem that the more erudite of them mention in their prayers.

"An interesting story, Shimon Peres. But I will confess that what interests me most is what it says about the emigration of Jews from Russia."

I understood why he said this. The massive influx into Israel of Jews from the former Soviet Union — a veritable unstoppable flood of humanity, and the most important and decisive event in Israeli history — symbolizes a victory, I was going to say *the* victory, if a costly one, for Zionism. This migration vindicates Herzl and his disciples, who were convinced that the question of the Jews could only be solved by the establishment of a national homeland, rather than by assimilation into Russian society or by embracing a revolution that promised to construct a classless society.

"In Vichneva and Volojin, and when I welcomed Jews from Russia in Israel, I began to grasp fully the state of affairs."

I told Herzl what lay behind this "great return." It began with the Russian Jews being humiliated by officials of the Ovir (the Soviet office dealing with visas). Their jobs were taken away from them and they were treated like pariahs and traitors by their fellow Soviet citizens.

These refusniks, some of whom perished in Siberian camps, have written one of the finest pages of contemporary Jewish history. As my friend Elie Wiesel has remarked, those whom we wrongly called the "silent Jews" were in fact the most eloquent and most vocal advocates of the Zionist ideal. They were the ones who gathered together each year for the Simchas Torah (the festival commemorating the return of the Torah), in front of the Moscow synagogue, to sing and dance in the streets. On that day, all access to the building was blocked to traffic, and the scenes that took place there are weighty with symbolism. Guided by a dream centuries old, hundreds of them proudly, openly, and stubbornly proclaimed their willingness to fight against totalitarianism. Even before Solzhenitsyn and others made their voices of dissent heard, Russian Jews revealed to us the bitter reality of the Soviet Union: the Great Night was followed by all those pale mornings when rifles drowned the most beautiful dreams of revolutionary change in blood — and the boredom, the deathly tedium of a soulless society.

"I think I can explain all this better if you will join me in Jerusalem for the Friday meal. Joining us at the table prepared for shabbat will be a Jew from the Soviet Union and the descendant of an old assimilated French Jewish family. To some degree both represent the solutions that over the course of the last two centuries society has proposed to the children of Israel: total integration into the status quo or embrace of change so radical that it would wipe Judeophobia from the face of the earth."

Herzl accepted my invitation to dinner, and we were joined by the Frenchman and the Russian, who, as always, found themselves in agreement on one point: of these two illusions — assimilation or revolution — the latter was the more difficult to combat. Liberalism, its theories of emancipation and assimilation based on the French model, had already collapsed during Herzl's lifetime. The Dreyfus affair had pushed him into writing *The Jewish State*, for it revealed the bankruptcy of this individualized approach to the Jewish question. The bourgeois societies that emerged from the Industrial Revolution proved incapable of being faithful to the words of Count of Clermont-Tonnerre, who announced in front of the French National Assembly, "We have to deny nationhood to the Jews, and we have to endow them everything as citizens." The idea was to refuse to see Jews as separate, or as enjoying a certain cultural autonomy and a distinct legal personality, yet at the same time not guaranteeing them equality before the law or freedom from the old prejudices. Just the opposite, in fact. More insidious, more cruel, and more murderous than the old anti-Semitism, the new anti-Semitism (exhibited as much by the political left as the political right) erected new barriers between the Jews and their compatriots, and then bore down on those Jews who had already broken with their traditions and merged into the dominant culture. Herzl himself had known this new anti-Semitism. One could not find better French, German, Italian, Austrian, and British patriots than the assimilated Jew.

After listening to what his French colleague had to say, my ex-Soviet guest suggested we end the evening at a Tel Aviv café, so that we might meet with some Marxist Jews.

"That," he told us, "would be a way to revisit the century that has passed, and to engage in polemics with those who still believe that the Communist revolution resolved the Jewish problem — that Communism relegated both anti-Semitism and Judaism (the source of all the ills Jews have suffered) to the trash heap of history. There were more of them than one might suspect. I do not exaggerate when I say that these illusions caused one of the greatest tragedies Judaism ever endured."

My Russian friend had no difficulty demonstrating that in the place of Sabbatai Zevi*and other false messiahs through the ages came the proletariat, raised to the ruling class — and that for entire generations of young Jewish revolutionaries, Marxist texts took the place of the Talmud. Having to choose between the universal and the individual, these Jewish intellectuals opted for the universal, or at least for a truncated form of the universal. Rejecting the idea of a "chosen people," and unconsciously yearning for individuality, they adopted the role of "salt of the earth," agents of world revolution agitating for the working classes. In essence, they adopted the theories of Karl Kautsky, one of the most famous representatives of Austro-Hungarian Marxism and a contemporary of and adversary of Herzl's, whom he criticized in these terms:

---

* A seventeenth-century Jew from Izmir who announced he was the messiah, and who gained an enthusiastic following within Jewish communities in Europe before converting to Islam and ending his days in Albania. His disciples followed him into apostasy and gave birth to a crypto-Jewish sect of "dönmeh," many of whose members played an important role in the Young Turk movement at the beginning of this century.

The danger run by Jews attracted to Palestine by messianic hope is not the only pernicious effect of Zionism. Even more dangerous is that they waste their fortunes and resources by going in this wrong direction, at a moment when their true destiny is being decided on an entirely different level, and which demands that they concentrate all their forces.

"I have heard enough," Herzl said with some frustration, having not been able to get a word in edgewise all evening long.

"Had any of you bothered to read my works you would have seen that nothing you are talking about is new. When I went to Russia to negotiate with the czar's ministers, I saw thousands of young Jews giddily caught up by the revolution. They were convinced they were fighting for the betterment of themselves and their families."

He went on to say that those most sensitive to Jewish cultural and linguistic identity had in 1897 (the same year as the Congress of Basel) created the Bund, the party representing the interests of Russian, Polish, and Lithuanian Jews who were proponents of a Jewish cultural autonomy based upon the Yiddish language, and the maintenance within the socialist society that was to come of a Jewish nationality with its own distinct political identity. (We tend to forget this today, but the Bund was the biggest and best-organized worker's movement in czarist Russia — far more active and influential than the Social Democrat Party, out of which came the Mensheviks and the Bolsheviks.)

Unlike the Bundists, Lenin's followers did not believe in the legitimacy of Jewish nationalism. When the Great Night arrived, Jews would need to join with the proletariats in the avant-garde of the working class — but as individuals, not as a people with a separate nationality. They must if necessary ignore the suffering of their people. After all, these sufferings were like a drop in the ocean of tears that had drowned all of humanity. Thousands upon thousands of young Jews would have taken to heart the admonitions of Rosa Luxemburg, a Polish Jew who became a mythic figure in the German worker's movement, admonitions she had directed toward one of her friends in a letter. The friend was trying to draw world attention to the Russian pogroms:

> What is the point of the particular suffering of the Jews? I myself am as touched by the plight of the miserable victims of the hevea plantations in the Putumayo region, or the Negroes of Africa whose bodies the Europeans bounce around like a ball. . . . I feel at home in the greater world, wherever there are clouds, birds, and tears.

"To the czarist authorities, the virulent anti-Semitism being promoted by extreme right-wingers within the Russian population was a consequence of the fact that so many Jews had joined the Russian revolutionary movement," Herzl explained. "That is what Count Witte pointed out to me. Let me read you this passage from my *Diary*":

"It must be admitted," he said, "that the Jews provide reasons enough for hostility. They are characteristically arrogant. Most of them are poor, and therefore dirty and repulsive. They engage in the vilest pursuits, such as pimping and usury. So the friends of the Jews find it very hard to come to their defense."

I thought to myself, how then do the enemies talk?

"Of late, a new and weighty factor has been added: the participation of the Jews in the revolutionary movements. While there are only seven million Jews among our total population of 136 million, they comprise about fifty percent of the membership in the revolutionary parties."

"To what circumstances would Your Excellency ascribe this?"

"I think," he replied, "that it is the fault of our government. The Jews are too oppressed. I used to say to the late Emperor Alexander III: 'If it were possible, Your Majesty, to drown the six or seven million Jews in the Black Sea, I should be perfectly satisfied. But if it isn't possible, we must let them live.' And that is my view still. I am opposed to any greater oppression."

I noted that Count Witte's "We must let them live" seemed eerily similar to Voltaire's "We should at least not burn them," a line from one of his anti-Jewish tirades in the *Philosophical Dictionary*.

"The czarist government," Herzl continued, "was using the growing numbers of young Jews in the Russian workers' movement — which had demonstrated with such violence during the 1905 Revolution — to justify both its anti-Jewish policy and the atrocities being committed."

Herzl admitted that he was no revolutionary. In fact, he was almost of the belief that Zionism would stem the growth of socialism within the Jewish population — as were some officials with whom he spoke in Russia. In *The Jewish State*, he dealt with the difficult position of Jews in modern times: the accusation that they were behind both capitalism and revolution at the same time.

The former Soviet at dinner with us told Herzl that he could not have foreseen the enormous upheaval brought about by the Russian Revolution, and how the birth of the Soviet Union was perceived by its followers as a proletarian Promised Land. Jews within the former Russian empire threw their support behind the new country, particularly since the White Russians and Cossacks and Ukrainian anarchists had massacred so many thousands of shtetl inhabitants.

"To the Jews, therefore, the Bolsheviks and their Red Army appeared as saviors."

To help Herzl better understand the Jews' enthusiasm, or at least one good reason for it, I recommended he read those wonderful stories by the great Jewish Russian novelist Isaac Babel. Babel was a friend of André Malraux's and a victim of the Stalinist purges. In *Red Cavalry*, he describes a competition between a Jewish mother and her son-in-law who are in disagreement over what name to give the son he and her daughter are expecting. The mother-in-law wants to name him "Yankel," a Yiddish diminutive of "Jacob"; the son-in-law wants to name him "Karl," in homage to the author of *Das Kapital*. In the end, the poor child is given the name "Karl-Yankel." There are thousands and thousands of "Karl-Yankels" among Russian Jews, who in 1918 became a nationality, like the Ukrainians, Belarussians, Russians, Tatars, Volga Germans, Georgians, and Uzbeks.

During the 1920s and 1930s, when few yet saw that the Soviet Union had given birth to a new form of totalitarianism, communism maintained its hold over the Jews.

*

*   *

There were no Communists in my native Vichneva. The Party was forbidden. To the Jewish inhabitants of the town, so deeply attached to their multisecular traditions, embracing communism was tantamount to converting to Christianity — it was outrageous, sacrilegious, unthinkable. This was however not the case in medium-sized or large cities in which there was a sizable Jewish population. There the Communist Party actively recruited former yeshiva students, those disillusioned by Zionism, and idealists. Communism exerted a powerful attraction, despite the gristmill of sameness into which the Soviet Union had thrown the Jewish people. Jews were permitted their own language, Yiddish (or at least one of their languages, since Hebrew was forbidden). But in exchange they had to renounce all nationalistic aspirations, and melt into the grim sameness of Soviet life, where the works of Marx, Engels, Lenin, and most of all, Stalin would govern their hearts and minds.

Stalin, the author of a weighty treatise on the subject, had decreed that every nationality needed its own territory. At the end of the 1920s, the Jews were given a Jewish state: an autonomous Jewish region, located between Siberia and the Chinese border, called Birobijan. Few Jews were willing to go there; most who did were liquidated during the great purges of 1937 and 1938. Birobijan was celebrated by dedicated Jewish Communists as the Promised Land, relegating Palestine to the trash heap.

Devouring its own children, the Revolution, as Nordau and Schnitzler had predicted, blamed Jews and Judaism for the sins of both Russia and Israel. During World War II, hundreds of thousands of Soviet Jews were massacred by the German *Einsatzgruppen*, as well as by their Ukrainian, Belarussian, and Baltic collaborators.

Following the German surrender in 1945, Jewish survivors believed that the indescribable suffering they had endured, as well as the heroic parts they had played in defeating the Nazis, as partisans and in the Red Army, would be recognized. Not so. Infuriated by the show of support during Golda Meir's visit to Moscow's great synagogue, and despite the fact the USSR had supported the creation of Israel, Stalin unleashed a vicious campaign against "cosmopolitanism." The "cosmopolitans" were essentially Jewish intellectuals; within hours they were arrested and sentenced to death. The campaign culminated in 1952 and 1953 with what was called the "White Coat" affair mounted by Beria, the head of security, and his cohorts. The Kremlin's doctors, among whom were a large percentage of Jews, were accused of planning to poison Stalin and other leaders, a plot hatched by "international Zionism." A carefully orchestrated press campaign degenerated into anti-Jewish psychosis. The Soviet secret police had prepared "spontaneous pogroms." Jews were deported "for their own good" to Siberia.

The intensity of the campaign can be measured in Mikhail Gorbachev's memoirs, in which the father of perestroika and the man who unwittingly brought down the Soviet empire describes an event during those grim months in 1952 and 1953 that created the first crack in Gorbachev's rock-solid belief in the Stalinist model:

An event in the winter of 1952 – 3 had a particular effect on me: the so-called "White Coat" affair, a pretext for anti-Semitic excess and for indiscriminate accusations of treason against the Jews. One day my friend Volodia Liberman, who had fought in the front lines during the war, didn't appear for the first class of the day. He arrived several hours later, looking exhausted and depressed. I had never seen him in such a state. It was as if he had come apart. When I asked him what had happened, he began to cry. He told me he had been thrown off a trolley car by a mob and then had insults heaped upon him. I was more shocked by this than I could possibly say.

Gorbachev never forgot his shock; it partly explains the lenient attitude he adopted toward Jewish emigration when he came to power. Emigration was a subject we discussed on many occasions, and on which he displayed a stunning independence of mind and gritty humor. The last time we met he asked me about the politics of the Soviet emigrants to Israel. I told him they tended to vote on the right. "There's something else they'll blame me for," he replied.

History will show that the Zionist movement did not need to wait for perestroika and glasnost to see the flaws in the Communist system, and to formulate a response to the legitimate demands of Soviet Jews.

"For as long as I can remember," I told Herzl, "I was convinced that communism would crumble, and that we in Israel would be joined by all our Jewish brothers and sisters, from Warsaw to Vladivostok, from Odessa to Tiranë, passing through Budapest, Sofia, Bucharest, or Addis Ababa."

I explained that I owed my conviction to two men, Berl Katzenelson and — once again! — David Ben-Gurion. The former was a prominent figure in socialist Zionism whom I met at the end of the 1930s. He had come to give a series of lectures on Zionism and communism to our little school at Ben Shemen. Unlike many others on the left, Katzenelson did not mince words about Stalin, who he compared to Pharaoh for having turned the "Soviet socialist paradise" into the "biblical house of servitude." To those who were bragging about Soviet projects such as the White Sea canal or the hydroelectric plant at Dnipropetrovsk, he replied that many of the enormous projects undertaken in Russia were like the Egyptian pyramids: their goal was to impress the people, not to benefit them. When, much later, I read in Solzhenitsyn's *Gulag Archipelago* about how the great utility of the gulag system was to educate workers, I realized how absolutely right Katzenelson was.

I trace to Katzenelson my having learned that Stalin was a despot who ruled by terror. Lies, murders, and impoverishment were the means by which the Soviet system retained its power, and Stalin's cult of personality was nothing but a gigantic screen that hid the truth from people. They had chased out God, Katzenelson thundered, and replaced him with a divinity of flesh and blood, a bloodthirsty and criminal tyrant. You cannot, he told us, get to "liberty by nonliberty" or to "nonviolence through violence."

"I became close to Katzenelson after this seminar," I told Herzl. "Today, when I walk through Mazeh Street in Tel Aviv, I can't help remembering the long Sunday evenings we used to spend in his apartment, surrounded by all of his books. We discussed how the vision of Zionism had been lost. He never passed up a chance to take apart Moscow's apologists and other sycophants of world revolution."

Indeed Katzenelson's assessment of the Communists could not have been harsher. If I dared to suggest that revolutionary utopias were driven by a great generosity, he was always ready with a reply: "Basic revolutionary fervor, which views radical destruction as the panacea for all social ills, reminds one of a child trying to prove mastery over its toys by breaking them."

Like Berl Katzenelson, David Ben-Gurion reinforced my hostility to communism, and my belief that it would collapse. He had read Marx and Lenin and admired the latter's leadership abilities. But he saw Marxism-Leninism as a totalitarian ideology and condemned the treatment of Jews in the Soviet Union. He was also no supporter of Marxism, and fought with those who wanted to fold it into the Zionist movement. One was Ber Borochov, the first theorist to attempt a synthesis between Jewish nationalism and orthodox Marxism. According to Borochov, were the struggle between the proletarian and the Jewish bourgeoisie to progress, what was needed was to concentrate Jews in Palestine, there to create a new society based upon the Marxist model in which the working class would rule.

For Ben-Gurion, this was simply plagiarizing an idea that was corrupt to start with. He had no intention of turning Jewish Palestine into a miniature Soviet Union. But his hostility to Marxism and to the USSR was not the product of circumstances. Like all true visionaries, he saw further than others. He knew that the Communist regime would eventually self-destruct, and that Israel would be there to welcome those Jews who escaped from the ruins.

I recall sitting in on a meeting between Ben-Gurion and General de Gaulle at the end of the 1950s. These two impenitent rebels, both capable of going against the grain of received ideas and the supposed lessons of history, had much in common. De Gaulle, for example, always said "Russia" instead of the "Soviet Union," believing that the Bolshevik system would be guided by the Russian spirit. He asked Ben-Gurion what was his fondest dream. The migration of millions and millions of Jews to Israel, replied the old lion. De Gaulle seemed surprised by this. He tried to argue that American or French Jews, or any Jews living in the free world, would never leave their homes to settle in Israel. It took more than that to dissuade David Ben-Gurion. He replied to the former leader of Free France that Israel would always be able to count upon the enormous reservoir of Jews living behind the Iron Curtain.

*

*   *

"At the time it was only a wish," said I to Herzl. "Today it is a reality."

Beginning in 1967, the appeal of Jewish nationalism has inspired thousands and thousands of Jews to seek visas to emigrate to Israel. We have all witnessed this unprecedented phenomenon, exceeding all expectations and demonstrating that the Jewish spirit somehow has survived the stifling weight of totalitarianism. Jewish migration from the Soviet Union was accelerated by perestroika and glasnost, the precursors to the collapse of the

Soviet system — a collapse that might well have had disastrous consequences for Jews.

Today, as we look at interethnic strife in Russia, in the former Soviet republics, or in the countries within the former Eastern bloc, we can see that the Jewish populations in these areas were in mortal danger. What happened to minorities living in Bosnia, Chechnya, and the Caucasus could easily have happened to them: victims of the terrible resurgence of rage within countries where for too long war and chauvinism distracted their majority populations from internal strife. If there were no Israel to take in significant numbers of Jews from the former Soviet Union, one can only imagine what might have occurred.

I prefer not to dwell on this kind of scenario. Israel does exist and it can protect these people. I prefer instead to rejoice in the fact that for several years our country has welcomed and integrated hundreds of thousands of people, many of them ignorant of Judaism and Jewish history, but who are or who will be, by the time of their children or their grandchildren, as Israeli as anyone, and who will strengthen a Jewish state at peace with its neighbors.

Living in Israel permits me to witness this miracle each and every day, when I hear Russian being spoken in the streets, or when I see the schedules of flights departing to or arriving from Moscow, Kiev, Baku, Tbilisi, Warsaw, Budapest, and Odessa at Ben-Gurion Airport — something unimaginable even a decade ago. Now that the Jews from the former Soviet Union are finding their roots in Israel, it is time to reflect upon the fall of communism and on the validity of Zionism, which found a way of overcoming its inability to get all Jews to Israel. Like Berl Katzenelson, Léon Blum, and a few others within the socialist movement fiercely opposed to the Leninist and Stalinist models, Herzl and his disciples committed the sin of being ahead of their time. Who among intellectuals and leaders flirting with communism during the anti-Fascist struggle or during the Cold War took the time to think about what they were affirming, and about what the Zionist-socialists were saying? They weren't listening. They believed that progress would come from Moscow, not from Jerusalem. Nothing better characterizes communism than a gap between the system's lack of imagination and the imagination of those forced to submit to the system. Never has so grim a form of government created such brilliant, luminescent personalities. It is nothing less than revenge of man upon ideology.

Today, former Communist apologists are destroying whole forests to print their acts of contrition. They are all writing their mea culpas and their *Ashmanou, bagdanou, hatanou*, depending on their religions. I do not deny them their need to do this, late though they are. But I confess to thinking that Israel, which has already integrated nearly a million Jews from the former Eastern bloc countries and which will integrate many hundreds of thousands more, constitutes, more so than these *kinot*, these modern lamentations, the most stunning refutation of the

Communist system. There is the true gauge of Zionism — the only ideology of the twentieth century that has not failed. We might agree that this fact is sufficiently exceptional to deserve note. And to be meditated upon.

I turned to Herzl. "And I hope you draw from this some measure of joy."

7

RETURNING TO THE
BEGINNING

*T*he ideal place for Herzl and me to finish our voyage around Israel was the city of Tiberias.

"This may seem a surprising choice," I admitted to him.

"Yes, I thought we might have to go back to bustling Tel Aviv, or to Jerusalem for further reflection. But I'm sure you have your reasons."

"Well," I replied, "some may be tempted to say I have chosen Tiberias for personal reasons. My daughter Tsvia was born there shortly after the declaration of Israel's independence."

I went on to explain that I also had other reasons for choosing Tiberias, each one loftier than the one before. To begin with, the first kibbutzim were started not far from Tiberias at the beginning of this century; these kibbutzim were the spearhead of the Jewish national renaissance in Eretz Israel. I spent my youth in one of them. Another reason is a moving passage by the great French poet Alphonse de Lamartine. Recalling his voyages through the Holy Land during the 1830s, Lamartine had this to say about the city:

> Tiberias isn't even worth a brief glance — little more than a collection of muddy, ramshackle dwellings, several hundred in number, that look like Arabic huts made of mud and straw. We were welcomed in Italian and German by Polish or German Jews who had come to spend their final years in Tiberias, there on the border of their sea, in the heart of their cherished land — to die under their sun and to be buried in the land of Abraham and Jacob. To sleep on the bed of one's fathers! Proof of the inextinguishable love for country. To deny it is useless — there is a sympathy, a bond between man and the land that formed him, from which he sprang. How good and sweet it is to return to this place, there to lend one's own little dust to what is already there.

I wasn't quoting Lamartine by chance. He was the author of the monumental *History of Turkey*, in which he discusses the desire of so many Jews to return to the Promised Land. I love this passage for two reasons. First, had I met Lamartine in Tiberias, I would have greeted him as a "colleague." "You see," I explained to Herzl, "Lamartine and I were both foreign ministers of our respective countries. He was a favorite author of my good friend, the late president of France François Mitterrand, whose knowledge of Israel and the Middle East grew from having read travel narratives about these regions written by Chateaubriand and Lamartine. Those are reasons enough for quoting Lamartine — let alone the fact he evokes so beautifully and accurately the timeless bond between Jews and the land of their ancestors."

"I know that passage, Shimon Peres," Herzl said.

Then I remembered that in *Old-New Land* Herzl describes the arrival of his heroes in Tiberias, where they celebrated Passover. As their car approaches the city, they cannot contain their wonder:

> The vivid pageant reminded them of the Riviera between Cannes and Nice at the height of the season. Fashionable folk were driving in elegant little equipages of all kinds — mostly motor cars with seats for two, three, or four passengers. But old-fashioned wagons, drawn by horses or mules, were not missing. Along the lake shore the travelers saw cyclists, horseback riders, and gay strollers in the cosmopolitan mob that is so typical of fashionable bathing resorts. They were told that the medicinal hot springs and the beautiful situation of Tiberias attracted visitors from Europe and America who had always sought perennial spring in Sicily or Egypt.

The passage contains Herzl's response (Tiberias as luxury spa) to Lamartine's description of Tiberias (as muddy village); it also subtly provides his own translation of a sentence from the Talmud, in which it is written that Tiberias is the place from which, at the end of time, will come the redemption of the Jewish people and of all of humanity, "Misham atidim ligael sheneemar: 'Hitnaari meafar, qoumi, shevi'" ("From there Israel will be saved, for it is said, 'Wake yourself, rise up from the dust, sit down,'" Rosh Hashana, 31b).

Tiberias's historical role, as well as the part it is predicted to play in the future, are strangely disproportionate to the town's actual size. The third-century Talmud rabbi Irmya believed that the name "Tiberias" came from the Hebrew *tabbour*, meaning "navel." Rather than symbolizing homage to Emperor Tiberius, as is generally believed, Tiberias's name derived from its being located at the epicenter of the land of Israel, even of the universe itself. As if doubting himself, the good rabbi also provides a second possible etymology. *Tveria*, the Hebrew equivalent of the Roman "Tiberias," comes from *tov* and *reah*, which combined mean "beautiful view," an allusion to the splendor of the town's setting. From Tiberias one can see the Galilee hills melting into the peaceable waters of a lake. Irmya anticipates the sort of wonder Herzl's heroes feel when they arrive on the lake shore.

The Tiberias of today is far different from the way it was imagined by the author of *Old-New Land* — he admitted as much to me — but it retains its charms. Going there in the spring or summer is an experience, and Herzl, a great tourist of the Eternal, visibly enjoyed visiting this historic city.

"I understand why you have chosen Tiberias," he

told me. "This pleasant city is so closely linked to the Zionist dream in so many ways, is it not?"

I assured him it was.

In the evening, as we strolled along the lake shores, Herzl and I came across two shadowy figures rising up from the depths of history. Herzl had no difficulty recognizing these ghosts: one was Doña Beatriz Mendès, called "the Signora," and the other was her nephew Joseph, Duke of Naxos, foreign affairs minister to Sultan Selim. "It would seem," Herzl remarked, "that I have been surrounded by colleagues during this entire trip."

The Signora and her son were born in the Iberian Peninsula — that Jewish "vale of tears" — when the ultra-Catholic sovereigns Ferdinand and Isabella decreed in 1492 that the children of Israel should either renounce their faith or be expelled. Rather than convert, they chose exile. On August 1, 1492, just as Christopher Columbus was setting off for Cathay in his three little ships, hundreds of thousands of Spanish Jews were treading the road to exile, taking with them their meager belongings and the heavily ornate scrolls of the Law that had been housed in Spanish synagogues — themselves masterpieces of Moorish architecture. The luckiest Jews made it as far as North Africa, where they founded communities and preserved their language, a mixture of Castilian Spanish and Hebrew. Some went to Portugal, where the monarch had promised to protect them in exchange for huge sums of money. Even there, alas, six years later, they were all forced to convert to Catholicism; children were taken from their parents and placed into convents and monasteries.

Many "Silent Jews," as they called themselves, attempted to leave the Iberian Peninsula for more peaceful surroundings, and one destination was the Ottoman Empire. It was there that Doña Beatriz found refuge following a very long journey; her nephew, Joao Migues (later her son-in-law) arrived after her. In Constantinople Doña Beatriz's fortune and charm gained her access to the sultan's inner circle. Joao Migues, who had reconverted to Judaism under the name Don Joseph Nassi, became close to Süleyman the Magnificent, and to his successor Selim II, and worked with their ministers of foreign affairs. He was paid for his services by being awarded the title Duke of Naxos, thus making him the first Jewish aristocrat in modern times.

In concert with Doña Beatriz, Joseph Nassi struggled to help hundreds of Jews fleeing persecution in Italy and Spain settle in his fiefdom in Muslim-held Tiberias, where a silk and clothing industry was developing. In so doing, he raised the hopes of many within the Jewish world of his time, proof of which we can find in letters sent by certain rabbis. One, Rabbi Angelo Gallico, spiritual leader of the community of Cori, in Campania, described the enthusiasm of Nassi's followers in letters he sent to communities from which he was soliciting financial help. Many in his community, he wrote, had decided to leave Italy and heed the call of "noble lord Don Joseph whom the Lord has chosen to be given the land of Tiberias, which God chose as the signal and symbol of our redemption." Hundreds of Jews crossed the Mediterranean and braved innumerable dangers to reach Tiberias. The results were significant enough that Jewish chroniclers of the time gave them a prominent place in their writings. Such was the case with one of the first great Jewish historians of modern times, Joseph Hacohen of Avignon, who in *Vale of Tears*, a classic of Jewish historiography, indulged in hyperbole to describe the rebirth of a Jewish city in the land of Israel.

"I had hoped you would meet Doña Beatriz and Don Joseph in Tiberias," I said to Herzl. "You would be able to reassure them that their dream of a return of Jews to Palestine has been realized."

I then took Herzl to the small cemetery in Kinneret, located near the kibbutz of the same name. There lie the remains of a man whom historians and political scientists today have forgotten, Moses Hess. Hess was a remarkable man, both a precursor to Herzl and one of the most lucid thinkers in modern times on the Jewish question. By this point in our travels Herzl had become aware of the entire history behind the founding of Israel. He bowed respectfully over the tomb of Hess.

Moses Hess was one of the most surprising figures in the Jewish world and the socialist movement, two entities with which I am not unfamiliar. Born in Bonn in 1812 and raised by his grandparents, both orthodox Jews, this contemporary of Karl Marx — who called Hess "my Communist rabbi" — was one of the principle theorists of the socialist utopianism, and one of the founders of the first Internationale. Unlike Marx and his Jewish followers, Hess never gave up on the idea of a Jewish homeland in Israel.

In 1862 Hess published a remarkable book called *Rome and Jerusalem,* a powerful precursor to Herzl's writings. To Hess, the Jewish question was one of many aspects of the nationalist questions that had started to plague political life in the central empires of his time. Like the Poles, the Czechs, the Magyars, the Slavs, and the Serbs, the Jews hoped to find their lost independence; Hess evoked his reunion with his nation with great eloquence. He perceived no contradiction between Enlightenment and nationalism, between celebrating both Jewish singularity and universalism:

> The movement that carries us toward national realization does not exclude concern for humanity — on the contrary, it reinforces it. This movement does not so much represent a global reaction against universalism, as a reaction against those things that can hinder it and cause its corruption, a reaction against the leveling forces inherent in modern civilization and industry, whose mechanization of life threatens to stifle all original and organic faculties. . . . One could not oppose universalist tendencies so long as their aim is to create connective ties between the nations of the earth. Unfortunately, universalism has gone too far in matters of life as well as sciences, denouncing anything that might appear individual and creative. Modern life

would be weakened by the vapors of idealism and science, and by the dust of atomism that would accumulate, like a fungus on seeds, keeping them from germinating. It is against these threats that weigh upon the sacred principles of a creative life that, today, nationalist tendencies are fighting, and it is solely to oppose these destructive forces that I will call upon the highest powers of Jewish nationalism.

This message still burns brightly. Reading it, one might now better understand why I decided to take Herzl to the Kinneret cemetery and to Hess's grave.

"I'm afraid I will not be able to recite the kaddish," he said to me. "The truth is that my religious instruction was cursory. I have practically no memory of the religious courses I was given in Budapest by a doddering professor whom my friends and I ragged endlessly. But, Shimon, I will reassure Moses Hess, just as I did Doña Beatriz and Don Joseph, that his dream had become reality. He too can now rest in peace."

"I have one more grave to show you."

I had hoped that these great figures from the past, mysteriously and miraculously reunited in this place where the spirit breathes still, would gather before the nearby grave of the poet Rahel (1890 – 1931), whose works have soothed me and many other Israelis. No one could put the splendor of Kinneret or the lake of Tiberias to music more beautifully than Rahel. Her words came to me as we stood before her small tomb.

There, the Golan heights — you caressed them
by stretching out your hand —
intimately a serene and silent pause;
and there, venerable Hermon
in its radiant solitude
the whitened summit
sends to me the wind.
There, on the lake's shore, a small palm
its branches tousled
like a mischievous child,
tumbles over the bank, getting its feet wet
in the waters of the Kinneret.

And then Moses Hess, Doña Beatriz and Don Joseph, Theodor Herzl, and I recited "To My Country," another of Rahel's poems, and one of the most moving love songs ever for the land of Israel:

I have not sung you, my country,
not brought glory to your name
with the great deeds of a hero
or the spoils a battle yields.
But on the shores of the Jordan
my hands have planted a tree
and my feet have made a pathway
through your fields.

Modest are the gifts I bring you.
I know this, mother.
Modest, I know, the offerings
of your daughter:
Only an outburst of song

on a day when the light flares up,
only a silent tear
for your poverty.

And so here Herzl and I ended our long travels together
around an Israel now just past its half-century mark. Far
from the bustling cities, the lake of Tiberias provided us
a place for reflection and meditation. The only noise in-
truding upon our thoughts was the gentle lapping of the
water, symbol of life and prosperity. For one moment we
forgot the daily squabbles that are the lot of politicians. All
we heard was the water's murmur — tender, reassuring. A
brief moment, all too brief, of quietude and communion,
a moment of grace.

As night fell, a numberless crowd converged upon
the shores of the lake. Joining us were the millions and
millions who over the course of centuries have made up
the Jewish people — generation upon generation upon
generation. A nation is composed not only of those living
in the present, but of those past and to come. In the crowd
are the Zealots who lived in a Palestine under Roman
rule, the Essenes emerging from their sanctuary at Qumran, and the Sadduccees allied with Rome; joining us are
Flavius Joseph, the historian who won over Titus, and
Rabbi Akiba ben Joseph, the bard of the Insurrection of
135; and the partisans of the Kahena, the Judeo-Berber
queen of the Aurès, and the Marranos, who secretly celebrated Judaism in Quito or in Buenos Aires; and the
proud Champenois rabbis of the eleventh century, and

the poets from the Spain of three religions; and the Jews from distant China, and those from Vichneva; and the *hāsīdh* disciples of Ba'al Shem Tov and the clever *mitnagdim* of the Vilna gaon; and the German and Polish *maskilim* and the believers in neo-orthodox Samson Raphael Hirsch; and the inhabitants of the shtetlachs of Eastern Europe, the *mellahs* of Morocco, and the *harats* of Tunisia; and the proud aristocratic owners of private residences in Paris, London, Vienna, or Berlin; and the partisans for world revolution, and believers in assimilation; and the believers and the nonbelievers and the agnostics; those who proclaim their Judaism, and those who have forgotten their origins; and the survivors of the massacres at Worms, Trèves, Fez, and Sijilmassa during the Middle Ages, or the Warsaw ghetto in the modern age; and the uncountable victims of pogroms and of the Shoah; and the pious rabbis commenting forever on the Talmudic texts, and intellectuals absorbed by modernity and by new ideas.

It matters little who they are and what they think. They were all gathered at this vesperal hour to listen to Herzl recite this passage from the Bible:

"If I forget you Jerusalem, may my right hand be severed."

For one timeless moment the world was still, suspended between the past, the present, and eternity. In the grace of that moment, all was finally order, calm, harmony, peace, prosperity, and happiness.

Herzl murmured the words that came spontaneously to his lips at the opening of the Congress of Basel.

"If you desire it, then it will not be only a dream."

I replied, "This dream today has another name, the most beautiful in the Hebrew language — shalom, peace."

EPILOGUE

On the way from Tiberias to Ben-Gurion Airport, we heard that a wildcat strike had been called by the airport personnel, and as a result, all international flights had been postponed by a day. I felt somewhat ill at ease vis-à-vis my traveling companion, and in order to cover up my embarrassment I suggested to Herzl that we use the spare time we now had — brief as it was — to revisit the Negev and its capital, Beersheba.

I called the air force commander, and explained to him what had happened. Considering the prestige of the personality I was accompanying, albeit not a military man but way ahead of us all when it came to vision, I requested that a helicopter be put at our disposal, the only way of getting a bird's eye view of the Negev in the little time we had.

The commander had a brilliant idea: he would allocate a helicopter to us, and arrange to have it flown by the legendary pilot Uri, dubbed "the Herzl of helicopters." Tradition dictated that whoever displayed outstanding visionary skills was nicknamed "Herzl."

And indeed, Uri demonstrated the versatility of this type of aircraft in the air, on land, and on sea. According to one of the tales related about this fabled figure, on one of his flights at sea — after all he flew by the force of vision and not by the power of fuel — the helicopter ran out of fuel. Forced to perform an emergency landing, he alighted on a huge American aircraft carrier. The ship's captain, who was taken by surprise, approached Uri, and snapped, "What do you think you are doing on our territory?" To which Uri retorted without missing a beat, "I'm sorry, Captain, but I thought it was one of our ships!"

Uri, it appeared, was very happy to get an opportunity to meet his namesake. Not lacking in a sense of humor, he turned to Herzl and remarked, "I will now show you the land you doubtlessly envisioned when you made the statement that a people without a land is seeking a land without people. Here before you is a land without people. . . ."

The large bird painted in bizarre khaki colors took off, and Herzl's amazement knew no bounds. "It is not only a different means of transport," he said, "it is another world. When on foot, the world appears to be one way, from horseback, another, and from a helicopter, the view is a sheer revelation. Every altitude," he added, "is a world of its own."

Uri decided to start the voyage by flying across the

wider part of the Negev, from the Mediterranean to the Dead Sea. "It is vital," he explained, "that Herzl behold the barrenness." As though to prove his point, the landscape that unfolded beneath us was one of harsh mountains eroded by metal-colored streaks of rust and bronze, from which emanated an atmosphere of utter desolation, separated by parched wadis glinting modestly here and there. "Something happened to the Almighty," exclaimed Uri, "when he fashioned the Negev. He was obviously under the influence of a strange and gloomy kind of mood, which affected his work, and he created a tortured stretch of land, constituting a challenge hard to ignore, and hard to tackle." The Dead Sea was already discernible in the distance, fragmented by canals of potash, the most important raw material that Israel possessed. Herzl was intrigued by the massive buildings down below, punctuated by tall chimneys jutting out from their roofs, as well as by the opulent hotels he could see lining the shore, and wondered whether they were interlinked. I explained to him that they operated in different directions and saw things from contrasting angles. The complex of large buildings along the Dead Sea's coastline, near the doomed biblical city of Sodom, belonged to the potash manufacturing plant. And further down, standing on its own, was a magnesium production factory, established with the participation of a German car manufacturing company. The use of this delicate metal, ductile and light, could become instrumental in the production of lightweight cars and cutting down on fuel costs. While these industrialists look upon the Dead Sea as a supplier of raw material for their production purposes, the classy hotels, whose object it was to encourage health-oriented tourism, in view of the renowned therapeutic properties of the Dead Sea for health care activities, see it as a vital source of tourist attraction. There is a big gap between the perceptions of the industrial sector and the tourist industry, for the latter claims that its trade spawns not only money, but peace as well.

Herzl was curious about the reverberating whiteness of some of the mountains, the brilliance of salt. I confirmed that these were indeed mountains of salt, and remarked that he surely remembered the story of Lot's wife, who was turned to a pillar of salt when she turned her head to look back at Sodom. Salt, since then, serves as a warning to all those who wish to look backward.

At this point Uri took a southward route. Herzl looked down on the Arava plain that stretches between the Dead Sea and the Red Sea. He inquired whether this strip of land held any particular interest, and I explained that it was here that the border between us and the Kingdom of Jordan ran. This prompted him to ask, "Where then are the characteristic signs of the border — barbed wire and minefields?"

I replied that what he was observing was an experiment at forging a new kind of border between us and our neighbors — one that did not serve as a declaration of enmity, but a border that would serve to promote opportunities for constructive cooperation between our two peoples. "For instance," I added, "we reached an agreement with the Kingdom of Jordan that at the southern tip of the border we would build a joint airport; one of its terminals would service tourists to Israel, and the other, tourists to Jordan. We are also planning joint railway tracks and who knows what else? Maybe a north-south canal will cross the Arava, transforming its landscape, with cross-border industries sprouting in the area, cementing closer relations between the two peoples." And I continued, "A hotel situated on the border between two countries can ensure more security than a military outpost, for it generates goodwill on both sides, by means of the stability and spirit of cooperation created."

Herzl concentrated his gaze on the settlements scattered the length of the Arava, and was curious as to their function. I explained that these were kibbutzim and moshavim populated by real idealists, who had declared war on the wasteland. "Make no mistake," I added, "the desert is a grim and deceptive enemy who does not surrender easily. But neither is the faith of the settlers placed lightly." I pointed to a particular settlement clinging to the side of one of the mountains in the plain, and recounted how it had been established by professors, engineers, and artists who had left the big city, Jerusalem, of their own free will and settled here. They were moved by the desire to seduce the wilderness, in a bold attempt to nurture it and watch it flourish and bloom with flowers, fruit, trees, and verdant growth.

Elat came into sight from the helicopter's front

window, glistening and exuberant, teeming with elegant hotels and sidewalk cafés. Because of the intense heat, women clad in minimal bathing suits were enjoying the coolness of the clear blue sea, and vivacious children were frolicking in the waters, thrashing about in the unthreatening waves. Elat is a city that has become renowned as one of the most attractive tourist centers in the region, and possibly in the world.

We did not have the time to land in effervescent Elat, and Uri therefore turned back north. We crossed the beautiful development town of Mitzpe-Ramon, observed the new military camp whose objective it was to train IDF officers for their future tasks, and admired the formidable sculptures molded in nature itself, set in the breathtaking scenic landscape, by artists whose hearts had been captured by the region.

Uri, seeming to read my thoughts, asked whether we would like to land in Sde Boker, near the grave of David Ben-Gurion. "Of course," was my immediate reply. He made a gentle turn to enable us to see the Sde Boker kibbutz, its peach orchards, the modest bungalow in which Ben-Gurion spent the latter part of his life, the school established in his memory, and naturally, the impressive Nahal Zin (Zin stream). Secluded from the other landmarks in the area, the wadi is a glorious and unique work of art created by the Almighty. Its primeval beauty has as yet not been blemished by the hand of man.

The helicopter landed in the vicinity of the grave.

The people who watched us stride across to the site rubbed their eyes in amazement at the sight of this elegantly attired man, boasting a thick black beard. Even here, in the middle of the desert, Herzl was still meticulous about his appearance.

While we were still making our way to the touchingly simple grave, we suddenly saw from afar a man clad in plain khaki clothes, marching along briskly. There was no room for error: he was striding in our direction.

Before I had time to say a word to Herzl regarding the person who had appeared so unexpectedly, Ben-Gurion had already approached him, arm outstretched, and said, "Welcome to the Negev." I whispered hurriedly in Herzl's ear that this was the legendary Ben-Gurion. He queried in a whisper, "Why is he dressed in these khaki clothes that have not even been ironed?" I failed to reply, for David Ben-Gurion beat me to it, and declared, "I am aware that you are the founder of Zionism, but we must define Zionism. Those who do not immigrate to Israel are not Zionists. The proof of your vision is in its very realization. Do not let anyone brandish the name of your vision falsely." Herzl barely stopped to absorb what Ben-Gurion had said, and asked, "To what are you referring? The whole of the land of Israel, or only the land of the Negev?"

Ben-Gurion again took the initiative and said that Israel was densely populated, noisy, and talkative. "Today," he continued, "true Zionism can only exist here, in the

Negev. In the Negev, a Jew can again be a Zionist pioneer, and possibly even a pioneer scientist." And then he added, "Our future depends on two things: our being a unique people, and a light unto the Gentiles. A people with moral values, whereby justice dictates policy, and truth sets the tone. We were born to be a moral people. Without a commitment to our moral heritage — and the vision of our prophets — we will not be able to survive. And since we are poor in land and rich in desert, we have to live on the strength of our scientific innovations, our technological skills. To till the land is not sufficient; we must also excel in science.

"The Jewish people, in its delivered land, must uphold its moral values and promote scientific accomplishments."

Herzl did not quite know how to act in the face of the overwhelming enthusiasm of this person, whose words gushed out with the force of a powerful torrent. David Ben-Gurion, without giving Herzl the chance to reply, led us to the Institute for Desert Research. We were shown thornless sabras (prickly pears), fish bred in practically no water, plants, and a variety of crops not to be seen anywhere else. "When it was necessary," commented Ben-Gurion, "we overcame enemy armies, even though they outnumbered us and were better equipped than us by far. The IDF has proven that we are able to defeat armies larger than ours. The time has come to challenge the wilderness, and conquer it in spite of the disproportion between us. Thousands of young people and throngs of new immigrants will converge here, in the Negev. They will discover that the desert climate is dry and very pleasant; and that there is no reason to be intimidated by bare mountains, but rather seek the means to exploit them by the use of creative ideas."

David Ben-Gurion informed Herzl that we will be producing electricity from the energy of the sun; the sun will compensate us for the lack of oil, and seawater desalination will make up for the inadequacy of the Jordan River — the famous and forlorn river in which history flows in greater quantity than water. He also said that he was sure high-tech would replace extensive agriculture, and that it would yield rich harvests and foster unprecedented prosperity. To this end, continued immigration was crucial, and the successful absorption of the newcomers vital. "We shall become one people, governed by true democracy. We shall change the election system, and reinforce the foundations of the state."

To Herzl's ears, these statements seemed strange and remote. He commented to Ben-Gurion that in his view, Israel needed to polish its infrastructure and improve its manners. To which Ben-Gurion retorted that to see a desert bloom was the most polished of all architectural accomplishments, and that values were more important than refinement.

David Ben-Gurion insisted we join him for lunch in the kibbutz dining room. Herzl did not quite know what to expect, but I gently persuaded him that such an experience would be worth his while. We entered the dining room. Everyone there was dressed in wrinkled khaki or working clothes. People stood in line holding trays, waiting to select the food they wanted.

There could be no greater contrast than the one that existed between these two personalities — David Ben-Gurion, clean shaven and his head crowned with a ring of white hair, as opposed to Herzl, whose hair was as black as a raven, and whose face was covered by a stately beard. Ben-Gurion was sporting an unbuttoned khaki shirt, whereas Herzl was dressed in a three-piece suit. David Ben-Gurion was wearing shoes dusty from the walk, while Herzl's shoes were still as highly polished as when he had left the hotel. Ben-Gurion had no patience for small talk, and Herzl chose his congenial words discriminatingly, to fit the present occasion. Ben-Gurion exuded the heat of the desert, and Herzl the aesthetics of Vienna.

Herzl reflected on the Congress of Basel, in which the poorest of the delegates wore a tailcoat, while Ben-Gurion talked of muscular pioneers wearing shorts.

Herzl reminded Ben-Gurion that it all started in the Diaspora, amidst the people in the provinces, in the shtetl, who placed their faith in the Zionist vision. Ben-Gurion rejoined that the offspring of these people were today outstanding soldiers and pilots, as well as scientists of the first order. "We have a new agenda," he added firmly.

Herzl was seized by nostalgia, and mentioned the bitter suffering of the Jews of Europe, whereas David

Ben-Gurion was only prepared to consider the vision of the prophets, or to be more precise, the prophecies that had still not been realized.

Ben-Gurion asked Herzl which part of Israel he had visited, and what he had managed to see. But before Herzl could answer, Ben-Gurion insisted that he had to visit Beersheba, the capital of the Negev, and Dimona, an amazing settlement town created from nothing by North African immigrants. And with a wink, he added, "Possibly Shimon might want to show you something else out there as well."

Toward the end of the meal, Herzl remarked somewhat ironically, but with a tinge of genuine enthusiasm, "The best part of the meal, Mr. Ben-Gurion, was its simplicity." We parted from Ben-Gurion, who said unexpectedly, "As long as the Negev will be a dead desert, my vision will be fueled with life." Herzl remarked politely that he had witnessed so many surprising events in modern Israel that he was confident Ben-Gurion's dream would become a Zionist reality too.

When we returned to the helicopter, Uri switched on its powerful engines, and a heavy cloud of sand obliterated the sky. We arrived in Beersheba twenty minutes later. From above, the city appeared to be spread out and uncongested; I explained to my traveling companion that the large complex of modern buildings we beheld was the Ben-Gurion University. I also pointed out an imposing building in the center of town — a shopping mall (upon his request, I elucidated that a shopping mall was a modern consumer's church), as well as a cluster of buildings at the periphery of the town, known as the Sarah Valley, constituting a state-of-the-art industrial park. I told him that the city had absorbed thirty thousand new immigrants from the former Soviet Union and that they had made a significant contribution to the industrial and scientific activities of the town. Beersheba, once the city of Abraham, was fast developing into an advanced scientific center.

The helicopter pointed to the east, and in no time we were able to see the silver dome and chimney of the nuclear reactor near Dimona. Herzl asked me when it was built, and what its purpose was, and I replied that we had started building this nuclear reactor, and all the auxiliary plants, at the end of the fifties. Its purpose was to bring peace. Herzl could not understand the connection between a nuclear reactor and peace agreements, but solving the riddle for him was not a problem: when our neighbors will come to accept that they cannot destroy us, they, too, will choose the road of peace.

Herzl inquired whether the theory had proved itself, and my answer was immediate: "A peace process is under way. This is a fact."

When we flew back to the north, he was interested to know what I thought Israel's new vision would be, and I responded, "Eliminate the desert by turning it to fertile soil, remove the salt from seawater, uproot enmity from the hearts of men, and turn enemies into neighbors."

"If this is the case," inquired Herzl, "has the Zionist dream ended?"

"Heaven forbid!" interceded Uri. "It just climbed another step up the stairs. The reality of it is that a second floor was added onto the ground floor. You planned the first floor, and we are now planning the second one, which will be even stronger, more spacious, higher, will have more of a view, and will provide more options. It would have been impossible to build it without the Zionist foundations."

Herzl appeared to be tired but pleased. The helicopter crossed the sky over Jerusalem. I pointed to Mount Herzl, the location of Herzl's grave, as well as the graves of thousands of soldiers and officers that had lost their lives in battle. I turned to Herzl and said that the tombstone of the man of vision was placed alongside the tombstones of the young fallen soldiers, for were it not for their courage and personal sacrifice, this vision would never have turned to reality. Tears streamed down Herzl's cheeks. The helicopter landed at Ben-Gurion Airport, and Herzl said that he had just one more discreet question to ask. Since it appeared that both he and Ben-Gurion were no longer among the living, was there anyone to replace them? In reply to his query, I told Herzl that we were lucky to have had him and to have had Ben-Gurion. The former's vision was that of a people. The latter's vision was that of a state. As a result, we have a people, and we have a state. Their vision is peace.

THANKS

*T*his book was written with the help of Patrick Girard and Stéphane Menamou, both of whom brought to it their remarkable knowledge of its subject. I am indebted to them for sharing their erudition with me.

Aviatal Inbar's excellent comments helped me finalize the text. Emmanuel Halperin and Claude Sitbon offered me priceless advice, as much on substance as on style. Professor Rafi Walden added critical details. The very enlightened opinions of Aliza Savir and Nissim Zvili were invaluable to me.

I need to thank René Guitton, who saw this work through from genesis to completion. He never stinted in his efforts to make the book measure up to his high standards, and those of the anniversaries it celebrates — the fiftieth anniversary of the founding of Israel and the centennial of Theodor Herzl's "prophecy."

I need to acknowledge Jeannette Seaver, Richard Seaver, and Timothy Bent at Arcade Publishing for their help in preparing the American edition of this work.

I thank them all from the bottom of my heart.